ADAM & A...

Even in his earl...
original ideas that...
As with David Bowie and Marc Bolan before
him, it was only a matter of time before the
public woke up to the potential of the
underground hero in their midst.

Adam was thrilled when his album *Kings of
the Wild Frontier* smashed to success at the
end of 1980. He had worked long and hard on
the new sound and image that drew on tribal
art and western eroticism. Adam was hungry
for acceptance – but even he did not expect the
stream of hit singles, gold album, meetings
with royalty and politicians, and the mass
adulation quite so swiftly!

What are the secrets of the revolutionary
new sound of Ant Music? Who are the Sex
People who swept a quiet, sincere young artist
with stunning good looks and a penchant for
make-up into the maelstrom of stardom?

Top rock writer Chris Welch investigates
the rise and rise of Adam Ant and probes into
the character of this extraordinary new talent.
Here is the full illustrated story. Find out why
this year is the year of the Ant!

ADAM & THE ANTS

Chris Welch

Star

A STAR BOOK

published by
the Paperback Division of
W. H. ALLEN & Co. Ltd

A Star Book
Published in 1981
by the Paperback Division of
W. H. Allen & Co. Ltd
A Howard and Wyndham Company
44 Hill Street, London W1X 8LB

Copyright © 1981 by Chris Welch

Typeset by V & M Graphics Ltd, Aylesbury, Bucks
Printed in Great Britain by
The Anchor Press, Tiptree, Essex

ISBN 0 352 30963 6

Dedications

Dedicated to Adam, Gene Krupa, Hilary, Marilyne, and Arthur Askey.

CONTENTS

Chapter One

KING OF THE WILD FRONTIER

'Adam!' the girls scream and the boys shout above a thunder of drums. On stage steps the most beautiful, the most outrageously sexy love child since Elvis swivelled his hips back in Memphis, Tennessee, in the dim mists of rock history.

He advances on his audience, weighted down with rings, belts, buckles, and leather, and begins a slow strip tease that would put the average Soho stripper out of business. But nobody shouts 'Get 'em on' or off. Instead there is a stunned silence and fascination, as Adam Ant wriggles free from his clothing, like a pavement escape artist removing his chains of bondage.

As his slim, hairless torso is revealed, glowing under the spotlights, a mighty roar greets his sensuous daring, while laughing youths bellow encouraging cries of 'Wanker!'

It's pure narcissism, a break down of the old strictures on male and female sexuality. And yet it is done with a kind of innocence and naïvety that transcends the violence usually associated with rock 'n' roll sex appeal. This is family entertainment, zips and leather for peak viewing time. There is no threat, no danger. The animal sneer of the early Presley, the androgynous perversity of Ziggy Stardust is wholly absent.

Adam sways from side to side in a curious, almost clumsy peacock's dance in a public mating ritual that would be of keen interest to your average TV anthropologist. And the music, a motley mixture of native rhythms and rock riffs, serves to pay homage to this painted warrior with trembling lips, the Beautiful Savage of Urban Dreams.

'He's pure sex!' sighs a girl as the Ants blast through a string of hits that have transformed the pop charts during the cold and gloomy winter months of 1981. 'I can't keep my eyes off his face,' confesses a hardened rock critic, busy making notes in the stalls in readiness for his next abusive tirade. The entire audience relinquishes the comfort of the seating provided inside the vast Dominion Theatre, in London's Tottenham Court Road, to stand on tip-toe, stretch and stare vainly over the heads of the milling throng.

The vigorously dancing figure seems to develop an aura that snuffs out any trace of the rest of the band. All eyes are riveted on the chief Ant, as hands stretch out to touch his legs or throw him tokens of affection. Suddenly the lights go up, and the band and their leader quit the stage, exhausted by the climax of months of feverish activity.

The ecstasy slumps, the dust settles and in surprisingly orderly fashion the audience makes for the exits, gazing around at its own unexpected make up of mums and dads guarding ten year old sons and daughters, post graduate punks and rock 'n' roll tourists.

Some clutch their glossy pictures of Adam, and heavily thumbed programmes, as they head for buses, tubes and cars. One bunch of Adam converts stop off at a nearby restaurant. As they order lager and unspeakably bad curries, the suspicious and uncomprehending Indian waiter gazes at the pictures on the cover, of the boy with hands on hips and thrusting crutch, 'What is this – man or woman?' he sneers. The mysteries of the Occident need some explanation.

Pop music history is a series of cyclic events, as the wheels of fortune spin, and periodically send off showers of sparks and flashes. Each outburst is greeted with disbelief and surprise. It is hailed as a never-to-be-repeated novelty that shocks the populace and sends them into convulsions. Then the wheel spins some more and a new generation finds fresh young meteors to gaze upon in wonder while innocent bystanders proclaim, once again, the end of civilization.

But things were different as 1980, a grim and uncomfortable year, ground to a halt. The age of heroes had been officially declared dead. Punk rock had finished off fantasy and the whole rock 'n' roll myth in one mighty piss take. And the Great Recession was closing an icy grip around the throat of the record companies. Album and singles sales were spiralling downward after the boom years of the seventies. The effects of home taping took their toll; the ever increasing cost of records made them less attractive. And much of the novelty of rock music - the whole business of collecting records, going to concerts, wearing the badges, identifying with the artists, reading about their exploits, was beginning to pale.

Older fans moved onto the task of support- ing burgeoning families, and the punk rock boom had singularly failed to produce many stars sufficient to support record companies in the manner to which they had grown accustomed. Desperate searches went on constantly if not for a mega-star, then at least for a group or artist who was going to sell more than a few thousand copies now that the million sellers seemed a dying breed.

As usual, 'The Next Big Thing' that A&R men yearned to spot, was beavering away in obscurity, upheld only by a pitiful faith in his own right to be a star.

Would the kids scream once more? Hadn't the spirit of fanaticism, so essential to a healthy industry of fantasy, been exorcised by the priests of punk? After Jimmy Pursey and Johnny Rotten, how could pop ever support another teen idol? We should have known better.

Perhaps it had all been done before, but a misty eyed graphic designer called Stuart Goddard, was determined that it should all be done again, for his benefit. He wanted an action-replay, but under his own rules.

Marc Bolan, Gary Glitter, David Bowie, Roxy Music – they had all stuck to their glinsel and titter – so why shouldn't a man with courage, determination, artistic sensitivity and a severe case of acne?

All his predecessors in British pop had succeeded by allowing free rein to their artistic expression and their unashamed love of the bold, posturing aspect of the artist as idol, a focus point for young dreams and escapism. Perhaps they had tamed the beast in rock, but in doing so brought a release of tension and pent up frustration inherent in the confused process of growing up and finding an identity. Off with the strait-jackets of society!

The story of the transformation of Stuart Goddard into Adam Ant, and his sensational flight to stardom, is one of the most encouraging epics of recent times, if you are at all concerned with the singular importance of trivia in the lives of the masses.

For trivia is but one part in a complex network of life support systems that makes individual existence bearable in an increasingly oppressive and dangerous world.

If Adam, not to mention his industrious Ants, has brought balm to the people, then his importance is sealed and his contribution has been as essential as subsidised bus fares and school milk. The acceptable face of pop music then, is a positive social service.

It may be difficult for the average petrol pump attendent or check-out girl to attain fame and individuality. Adam has done it for them.

Adam did it for a whole spectrum of society during the first heady months of his rise and rise. Company directors were observed tapping secretive toes to the strains of 'Stand And Deliver'. Schoolboys flung off satchels and bicycle clips to rush to their bedrooms and daub their faces with white paint, scaring pet hamsters and elderly aunts in the process. School girls giggled, shrieked and wrote obscene letters to his fan club, inviting a shocked Adam to partake of unspeakable practices at prearranged rendezvous during half-term. Overweight and haggard rock journalists dashed out to buy typewriter ribbons and wondered whether 'Ant Fever' sounded better than 'Ant Mania'.

Industry might be going to the dogs, but the country was going to the Ants. Television and radio were swamped by an output of exciting new pop music that dominated the charts. There had been nothing like it since er – the

Bay City Rollers? Since Slade? No – not since the Beatles!

The Ants pop conquest began in summer 1980 when *Kings Of The Wild Frontier*, their July single release, broached the bottom end of the charts. It was followed by a whole spate of hits starting with 'Dog Eat Dog', 'Antmusic', the return of 'Kings Of The Wild Frontier' to the top of the charts, and 'Stand And Deliver'. The source of most of this material was his platinum album *Kings Of The Wild Frontier* which stayed in the charts for an incredible nine months. Whenever it showed signs of slipping, it promptly went up again. The singles and albums charts became a veritable Ant music catalogue.

But this sudden blitzkrieg was the culmination of several years of struggle and disappointment, when Adam had fought his earliest battles for recognition in the beer, spit and urine-soaked hellpits of the London punk rock inferno.

For Adam Ant was one punkrocker who learned his lessons, wiped the sputum from his brow and slowly fumbled his way out into the broad, sunlit uplands.

Adam was caught up in the excitement generated by the Sex Pistols in 1976, after he saw them playing at St. Martin's College of Art. His studies as a graphic designer naturally led him to investigate the artistic imagery of rock and to be intrigued, nay flabbergasted by the way the Pistols, albeit in a crude way, under the influence of their mentor, Malcolm McLaren, seemed to mimic and mock the lumbering rock tradition, like revolutionary artists sawing the legs off the easels of the great masters.

There was more pistol-whipping of society than sexual expression in the ferocious onslaught unleashed by John Lydon and Sidney Vicious Esq. but they sowed several seeds in the earnest young student, who had until then spent most of his time attempting to remove traces of burnt sienna from his national health glasses.

'I say you chaps,' he may well have squeaked, 'this beats tracing and painting by numbers into a cocked hat. I'm for forming a pop group. Anyone game?'

Stuart Goddard had inherited his mother's Romany good looks, even though the ravages of youth at one time seemed likely to endanger them. The family are proud and there is that defensive streak that comes from knowledge, indeed first hand experience of persecution. Adam knew that during the Second World War, the gypsies suffered under the extermination policies of the Nazis and his father, a tank driver in the British Army, had seen the results of that when he was among those who relieved and uncovered the horrors of Belsen prison camp.

The treatment of minorities is a theme that has cropped up many times in Adam's songs, whether Africans or American Indians, and it is this serious, considered and intelligent use of the pop medium which has ultimately given him much respect and credibility.

Stuart was born on November 3, 1954, and grew up on a council estate. However sensitive he might have been, he had an early grounding in the attitudes and needs of every day kids. Indeed he wasn't that sensitive for when he went to Marylebone Grammar School, he took up the none too gentle sport of rugby.

Like most of his mates, Adam was enthralled by the pop stars of the day, and he especially liked Marc Bolan and T. Rex. He actually met Marc and asked him for an autograph which he still treasures. It was an act of generosity that made Adam think that if ever *he* became a star, he would always give fans an autograph, and when fame came, he attempted for a long time to answer every fan letter, until he was swamped by the sheer weight of letters.

As far as schoolwork was concerned, Adam wasn't exactly a scholar. He most enjoyed playing rugby and it helped build up the famous physique and endurance for the long hours of performing, on stage, to come. He also tried his hand at playing the viola, one of the school instruments, and made his first attempt at singing, in a friend's band.

The years at school were not entirely wasted, for Stuart Goddard was presented with A-level certificates for History and Art, which helped him when the time came to step out.

As he absorbed the pop music currently in the charts he felt a growing affinity with Bryan Ferry and Roxy Music, and he went to see them performing at the Rainbow Theatre, in North London, in 1973. He was impressed by their stylish approach to blending manners, music, appearance and PR image. Some bands, particularly of the pub-rock persuasion, looked worse than their roadies after a hard night mucking out Four-be-Twos. Roxy, Bolan and Bowie were an aesthetic delight, despite the howls of 'Glam-Rock Bilge!' from purists, die-hards, and grumbleweeds.

Like many rock musicians before him, Stuart the grammar school boy decided to become an art student, and he entered Hornsey Art College. He was over half way through his graphics course when he saw the Sex Pistols, and he knew that music was going to be the strongest influence on his life, and art would have to be bent before its will.

While still at college though, he joined a band called Bazooka Joe, with his friend Danny Kleinman. One of the bands that supported them was the Sex Pistols!

He became more open in his tastes developing a fondness for Cream and the drumming of Ginger Baker, and listening to blues and cajun music.

Adam just couldn't see much future in spending his time writing theses, and didn't see how this would relate to his earning a living in the real world. But he was grateful for his art school training later when he began to do all the graphics for the Ants. Like his idol, Bryan Ferry, he was keen to place emphasis on attention to detail and keep up a high standard. When the time came, Adam would take care to control everything that related to him and his image.

So Adam quit Hornsey in early 1976, his life changed, he claimed, by the vision of the Pistols. He became a punk and rejoiced in the fact that you didn't have to be good to form a punk rock group. Indeed you didn't have to be able to play a musical instrument, such was the stripping bare of tradition.

The rock scene had grown top heavy with bands with star instrumentalists, many of whom had been to Royal Colleges of Music, and weren't far short of classical music standard. Drummers were brilliant, guitarists ran rings around even earlier wizards like Jeff Beck and Eric Clapton in terms of speed and dexterity. It was all getting too much and nobody else could get a look in. Just as rock 'n' roll's raw exuberance had overthrown the dance bands in 1956, so in 1976, exactly twenty years later, the old idols were overthrown, and there was a great trampling down of graven images – craven images in many cases, as they whimpered before the onslaught of vituperation, scorn and resentment.

Punk rock quickly created its own classics

and mythology, and hopping up and down on the fringes, desperate to be heard, was the ex-Stuart Goddard.

He wasn't going to be a cartoon character, like Atom Ant, but a hunk of jailbait, in black leather and chains, taking the Sex Pistol ethos a stage further into militarism and sado-masochism. Adam & The Ants made their debut at London's Roxy Club on April 23, 1977.

The impact of the Ants was considerable on the underground. His name was emblazoned on the leather jackets of every hard core punk. He was invited to appear in Derek Jarman's film *Jubilee* and recorded two of the sound-track numbers, 'Plastic Surgery' and 'Deut-scher Girls'.

His first gigs were disasters but few cared. Adam had credibility where it counted, and if the music press attacked him for being some kind of neo-fascist (which he hotly disputed), then so much the better. Audiences responded with that touching affection known only to the fraternity of punks. They threw bottles at him.

'Only five fans turned up to see us at one of our first gigs,' recalls Adam. 'We played at the ICA Gallery in the Mall, and we got in by telling the organisers that we were a country and western group. After they heard us, they threw us out, after one minute!'

Some of Adam's oldest fans have vivid memories of those pioneer gigs. Says Magenta, a rock publicist who works in Chelsea, and now handles such top names as Paul McCartney & Wings and Iron Maiden: 'I used to go and see Adam a lot in the old days, but I don't think he was nearly as good as he is now. But even then he was terrifically sexy. He wore black make-up and black bondage clothes from the Sex Shop in Kings Road, which nobody dared talk about much then. He wore tight black leather trousers with lots of zips and the audience was very freaky and heavy. To tell the truth, I thought it was all a bit of a joke.'

Indeed sex shops had already begun to display early posters of Adam in such garb, long before the general public became aware of the Ant in their midst.

Another fan, Graham, aged 25, from Colchester in Essex saw Adam at Colchester Arts College in 1977. 'He was supporting Siouxsie and the Banshees and he was playing total punk, just three chord stuff. He had his manager, Jordan, with him, and she sang some of the numbers.'

'Adam had terrible acne and long hair. Later I saw him in February 1978 at Chelmsford and he was absolutely brilliant, and had improved no end from the previous year. It was during the period when he was wearing a little kilt.

'There was a riot that night because the other band had brought forty supporters along from Brixton. Once their band, called

Void, had finished, they all went crazy. The police had to be called out to chuck 'em out, and they even used tracker dogs.

'Adam had a very heavy punk following, but his fans were not violent. By 1979 he was really the leader of the Underground. All the punks can't help feeling that he has sold out, but I say good luck to him. His *Kings Of The Wild Frontier* album was brilliant.'

One of Adam's younger fans is Ben, aged 15, from Kingston, Surrey, who never saw him in the old days, even though he followed all punk events and outrages. 'I was too young to go to the Vortex, or any of the punk clubs, but I heard all about him.'

Ben was attracted by the legendary figure, and says: 'It was such original music and he was totally different in his style of dress, from anything that had gone before. A lot of kids had heard about Adam, but probably only saw him for the first time when he appeared on telly. My first time was when he played at the Dominion Theatre. All the audience stood up and he was great. But I was disappointed when he just introduced each number. I thought he was going to talk more to the audience, about Antmusic and stuff.'

Like thousands of other new Ant People, Ben first heard Adam on his legendary *Dirk Wears White Søx* album, released on the independent Do It label on November 30, 1979.

'That was good,' says Ben. 'Wholly original

but wholly punk. Since then I think he has got a bit too commercial, and I didn't like him meeting royalty and going to Variety Club awards.'

Mark P., editor of the earliest punk fanzine, *Sniffin' Glue* was among the regulars at the Ants' Tuesday night gigs at the 100 Club. 'It was very exciting to be there. I remember one number that went "Shine A Beacon On A Puerto Rican," and Jordan came on for one number called "Lou". The Ants always had a lot of good tunes, and were a very musical band. I knew Marco in those days before he joined the Ants. He was in a band called The Models, and they recorded that single "Freeze" and "Man Of The Year" for Step Forward. This was in 1977. Marco was a really nice person. He was a bit big and tubby and spoke in a high pitched voice. Technically he was a very good guitarist. He was from Harrow, and his parents had an Italian restaurant in the West End.

'The thing I noticed about the band then was that their clothes came from the kids on the street and not from the designers. But Adam was developing his own style. He went for the Jim Morrison style leather trousers and he had black pencil lines coming from his sideburns onto his cheeks. He was never a political revolutionary. He was more involved in sexual politics and he appealed more to the hippie-punks, rather than the oi-punks.'

Those early gigs polarised opinion in such a

way that there is still a sharp division between those who think either the old Ants were much worse than the present band, or vice versa. Says Ian Birch, the respected rock critic, 'I hated the old Ants. I thought they were dreadful, until Adam had his rethink and took them away from that kind of pseudo-fascist stage act. I thought his act was not very pleasant. It was punk at its worst and a precursor of 'Oi' music. Adam was a Sex Pistols' camp follower, and he was lousy in the old days. I think he's much better as a pop star – and he looks much better!'

It was inevitable that, just as Adam had become influenced by his idols, Ferry and Bolan, that kids all over the country would soon adopt whatever new trend or fashion the Ant Meister presented for their delectation. It was a tradition that went back to Teddy Boys – and Cliff Richard – copying the Presley quiff, snarl and gold lamé jacket.

But says Ben: 'Some of the fans had very original ideas, and didn't just copy Adam. They painted zig-zag stripes down their faces, and didn't just wear the white streak across the face. Some put crosses on their eyes, and made up their hands, painting them completely white, and then adding patterns onto the white background. They paint anything that shows.'

The punks themselves, if they were feeling in an unusually charitable mood, hoped that Adam's success might make the old punk style more acceptable on radio and TV. The rest just cut out his pictures from every magazine and stuck them on the bedroom wall in time-honoured fashion.

But Peacock Punk was still but a fluttering feather in the future when Adam was dodging the spit and bottles on his way round the punk circuit. Marc Bolan had spent years in the wilderness of the late sixties underground scene, bopping with the hippies and Tyrannosaurus Rex, before *Top Of The Pops* beckoned with its skeletal fingers. And Adam too had to pay his dues and plot and scheme before he could become an all-sex entertainer.

Marc Bolan would have been proud of him.

There is something of the teacher in Adam Ant, *even* though he hates to preach. When he was still at grammar school he was so good at painting, he'd end up teaching the whole class, although doubtless his headmaster would have been alarmed if Adam introduced to them the delights of his favourite artist, Allen Jones, famous for his pictures of girls in stark black underwear.

Despite all the adverse press criticism, Adam always took his role as communicator with audiences seriously. He learnt early on that it was easy to influence, and how swiftly words, gestures and ideas could be passed on and absorbed.

More than a simple desire to attain pop star status, Adam was anxious to present his ever expanding audience with a whole package, a concept that would be perhaps more positive than the negative stance and nilhistic attitudes inherent in punk.

The Clash and Sham 69 were blasting kids with songs of violence, and sounding a call to arms. Adam was not impressed. But he still needed help, and was delighted when he finally came into contact with Malcolm McLaren, the Sex Pistols' manager, who offered to take Adam under his cloak when they met at a party.

McLaren was a hero to Adam, and it was mortifying when the manager suddenly dropped the lead singer and took the Ants of the day, Dave Barbe, Matthew Ashman and Lee Gorman, to form a new group called Bow Wow Wow. It was January 1980 and a turning point in Adam's career, that may have seemed like a disaster at the time. It led him on to greater glory.

Chapter Two

CRACK UP

Stuart Goddard underwent enormous pressures during his school years, as he groped his way towards freedom and artistic expression. Like most kids, he was torn between influences, teachers, friends and parents. His parents were divorced when he was young, and although he managed to get through the initial traumas apparently unscathed, the effects of rows at home seemed to surface when he was in his late teens and subconscious images began to rise and torment him. His father worked as a chauffeur and his mother worked as a housekeeper at the St. John's Wood home of Paul McCartney.

Little Stuart never got to speak to his idol but he did have a signed copy of one of McCartney's albums. Years later, when he took up the bass guitar, he was influenced by Paul's bass playing.

Stuart was always close to his mother and loved her sense of humour. But she was also strong willed and was once described by someone who had crossed swords with her as a 'Mrs Thatcher type'. While his dad was freewheeling, and happy go lucky, Mum was strictly orthodox in her views. She found it difficult to accept his pop star status and always nursed hopes that he would eventually settle down to a 'proper job' or return to his studies. Even while Adam was roaring up the pop charts, she continued in her job as manageress of a launderette in the same North London suburb where the family had grown up.

If Adam repressed his darker thoughts under her formidable influence, they were to find full expression in his songs and artwork when he tasted the heady wine of freedom at Hornsey Art College, and began to trans-mogrify into Adam Ant.

But Adam's emotional needs and driving ambition were sharpened by the sense of self-discipline instilled by a well-organised mother. He needed to prove his independence from home life, to cut free of apron strings, to do things his own way on his own terms.

This need was bound to lead to clashes later in life, especially when he met musicians and artists of similar drive and ego. Like all who seek independence, he knew he needed the help of others along the way. Adam needed people, care and understanding. He sometimes accepted help, but sometimes rejected it, leaving behind hurt pride, often exaggerated in the light of his subsequent success. He was to suffer much from the 'I taught him everything he knows' syndrome.

'My parents were divorced when I was about seven,' recalls Adam. 'My childhood wasn't too happy, but it's a bit tedious to talk about it now.' There were rows, of course, and these had the result of making him appear quiet and withdrawn at times. He had few girlfriends and sought solace in the therapy of eroticism. He thought that hard core pornography was incredibly dreary and unimaginative, but read books on the taboo subject of fetishism, which celebrated the wearing of leather and rubber clothing. In 1978 he wrote 'Rubber People' with lines like, 'Rubber people are lovely people, they long for latex beside their skins' and 'Gagged and disciplined, bound in bondage, least until this treatment ends, spanked in satin, whipped in Wigan, for they are our fettered friends.' The pun indicated he could see the funny side of this aspect of the human condition.

As an artist he appreciated the beauty of erotic images, and like millions of men the world over, was inclined to believe that 'certain clothing' enhanced the sexuality of beautiful women. When he met Eve, who was to become Mrs Eve Goddard at Hornsey Art College, he felt he had found a sympathetic soul, who would understand such matters.

They married in 1975 when Eve was eighteen and Adam twenty, but their marriage was kept secret for many years because it was feared that knowledge of Adam's marital status would upset his fans, and indeed it was quite likely that it would.

When news of their marriage was finally revealed in July 1981, Eve told how Adam was 'perfectly housetrained' by his mother, was good at housework and kept everything tidy. They started out as a very normal, happily married couple. But such domestic bliss must have seemed like a millstone around a young man's neck. It was all too soon after the family ties of childhood.

The strain began to tell, and he began to refuse to eat, and this developed into Anorexia Nervosa, the slimmers disease. He found it increasingly difficult to communicate. The dead weight of suburbia oppressed him because he understood it so well, and realised it could be a mind numbing trap. He gently mocks its preoccupations on his song 'Cartrouble' on *Dirk Wears White Søx* where he sings, 'I used to sit at home silently and wonder why all the preference is polishing the chrome while all the mothers and the sisters and the babies sit and rot at home.'

Whatever Adam did with his life, he was determined not to sit and rot. And yet Stuart Goddard, art student, did not make a great impression as a future sex symbol on Eve. But at first he seemed cheerful and attentive. 'He chased after me for months,' she said.

They lived in a rent-free flat next to her mother's home and they worked together on their art projects, and as they were both interested in fashion, Stuart asked her to design rubber stage clothes based on the ideas he drew from rubber-wear magazines.

It seemed an idyllic existence – Adam & Eve in a rubber-wear paradise.

But Adam's illness became so bad he took an overdose and went to hospital and was only released on condition that Eve looked after him. For six months she nursed him back to health. 'I was really fucked up in the head,' recalls Adam. 'Things went wrong and something snapped. I just became a vegetable for three months. I couldn't talk to people. I was very ill and that was part of the reason why I left college.'

When Adam was in hospital for psychiatric treatment he met so many mentally ill people it left an appalling impression on him, 'a scar on my brain'. His own nervous breakdown was not helped by a girl patient who walked into his room one day and relieved herself on his floor. It was not a pretty sight.

The crack up occurred during his final year at Hornsey, and he had reached the point where he had to choose between an art career and music. 'The two meant more to me than anything else,' he said. 'The conflict just wiped me out. When you have had an illness of any sort, you have to fight it every day for the rest of your life.'

After his illness Eve realised that Adam had changed and their marriage, once so happy and normal, was in danger. Eve had left college too, to look after him, and claimed she had missed out on the chance of getting several jobs as a result. But it was agreed they should live apart. At first they shared a flat, but had separate bedrooms. It was more like a partnership, and Eve did not object when Adam brought back new girlfriends, which naturally increased in number as his fame as a musician spread. She designed more stage clothes, and ultimately helped create the Adam Ant Look that was to create such a sensation within a couple of years.

Chapter Three

ANT ANTICS

The genesis of the Ants can be traced back to a legendary art school band called Bazooka Joe which featured guitarist and singer Danny Kleinman who later designed an Ant logo for Adam's Red Indian period.

Bazooka Joe started out in 1971 and was in the grand tradition of art school bands like the Bonzo Dog Doo Dah Band and Deaf School. They were on the same scene as Kilburn & The High Roads and the 101'ers, featuring Joe Strummer, later of Clash fame. The importance of such bands has been crucial to the development of British rock. The art schools led the way in fashions and concepts, and provided not only a melting pot of ideas, but created a perfect environment for students to rehearse groups, in between spasmodic attendance at lectures.

The Bonzos were one of Adam's favourite

bands and he particularly liked their *Let's Make Up And Be Friendly* comeback album. Bazooka Joe, like the Bonzos, often mixed old pop hits - in their case 'Pipeline' by the Chantays and 'Apache' by the Shadows - into their own original material.

Danny and Adam were both at Hornsey and the latter was quickly co-opted into the band on bass and vocals during 1975/76. Adam had taken up bass, under the spell of his childhood hero (another one) Paul McCartney, and also listened a lot to Jack Bruce and his work with Cream. He also started writing his own songs with titles like 'Quasimodo' and 'Brighton Rock'.

In the intermission Adam sometimes played a duo spot with his friend Dave Angel on acoustic guitar, when they sang Roy Rogers' 'Four Legged Friend' a cowboy song which they parodied for the amusement of fellow hedonists. 'It used to crack 'em up,' says Adam fondly.

Drummer Richard Wernham, now with the Refugees, was an early member of Bazooka Joe and says: 'I was at Orange Hill grammar school in Edgware and we formed Bazooka Joe with John Ellis. It broke up, then, Danny Kleinman on guitar started it up again. He's now a graphics designer, but he kept it going for a long while and Stuart came in on bass. They had a good following around Hampstead.

They were a semi-pro band and played goodtime music - a bit like Madness are now.

But it was more outrageous. There was a backing girl vocal group called the Lillets which was quite strange. Everyone dressed up and was influenced by that movie *Clockwork Orange*.'

Richard recalls that the band recorded 'at a big flash house in Stanmore' and the tapes would have featured Adam. 'But nobody thought they were significant at the time or took it seriously. Lots of people went through the band who have since become famous.'

One steaming night in 1976 Bazooka Joe played a gig at St. Martin's School of Art, in Charing Cross Road. The support band caused something of a sensation. They were called The Sex Pistols. The effect on Adam was devastating. Somehow 'Four Legged Friend' didn't seem so meaningful.

'As soon as I saw Rotten and he opened his mouth, I knew I needed something else. He was the man,' said Adam. When Adam saw Johnny Rotten snarling and sneering with the Pistols, he realised his sojourn with Bazooka Joe was over. He vowed he would form his own punk group and he called into creation the B-Sides, with one Lester Square, a fellow student, on guitar. Beyond occasionally raising his voice at the end of a lyric in the Rotten style (designed to disguise flagging wind), Adam was not an overt copyist. Instead he absorbed the energy, the fury and the dedication.

He had experience of leading a schoolboy

band while at grammar school, but the B-Sides were to go down in history as the progenitors of the Ants. There were desultory rehearsals, the band did not achieve much, and as there were virtually no gigs to be had, understandable frustration set in, and Adam split.

There is no more depressing situation than being in a half-rehearsed band playing to itself . . . without the sweet music of applause. Or even some beer money by the end of the evening. All great rock bands have been in the same situation at some stage in their careers. Only the most determined and talented survive.

The Punk Rock scene meanwhile had taken off to the extent that the Sex Pistols were headline news every day as their increasingly outrageous exploits stunned the public and shook up the music business who thought they were merely the new Rolling Stones. Record companies were ripped off, elder statesmen of rock abused, and the old principles of love and peace, still hanging over rock's thinking from the sixties, were finally buried in a welter of rage, cynicism and violence. It was like Mao's cultural revolution, when Red Guards poured scorn and criticism on their elders, and banished all progress. Scientists may yet prove that punk was indeed a distant echo of that strange upheaval in the Far East, as it sent ripples across humanity.

Punk rock had its own high-minded principles, a kind of working class puritanism, fuelled by spite and contempt. To a confused, but open-minded grammar school boy it must have seemed a trumpet call to revolution, and a key to unlock the chains of social bondage. Musicians, rock journalists and even a few turncoats from the rock establishment jostled for a place at the camp fires of the new punk army.

But as with all revolutions, ideals became soured, the sense of purpose and unity distorted and lost, and when Adam's band signed to CBS, the bastion of corporate rock, he was at pains to emphasise it wasn't a punk rock flagship.

He had endured quite a few grim and painful experiences at the hands of the more wild-eyed exponents and devotees of the punk movement. Not all of them saw nilhism or sado-masochism as aesthetic concepts or artistic images. He who rouses the mob does so at his peril, and the mob have a nasty habit of taking things at face value, and ultimately becoming more committed and dangerous than the leaders and sowers of ideas. Punk Rock became a way of life, a nightly ritual of violence and degradation.

Many who visited the punk havens like the Vortex and Roxy clubs in London's West End, expecting revelations of a new dawn, found instead sullen youths spitting on the bands in an orgy of revisionism. The anti-fans pogo-ing in the audience were the stars. The anti-heroes on stage were merely the accompaniment, to be used and abused. It may have been pure and important, but it was hardly pleasant. Adam later described the Roxy, with much feeling, as a 'shit hole'. And it was hardly surprising he felt so disenchanted for it was there one night that he experienced the excruciating pain of a man's fingers tearing the flesh from his back, as he attacked Adam unexpectedly from the rear. His finger nails digging deep, the assailant calmly explained that he thought Adam would approve of this gesture. He was simply joining in the bondage stage act. It was all a far cry from the secret pleasures of magazines arriving in plain brown paper wrapping through the letter box.

Adam was a trouper however, (like Arthur Askey) and the show had to go on - for as long as he could stand the pain.

The first Ants band consisted of Lester Square (guitar), Andy Warren (bass) and Paul Flanagan (drums). It was early 1977 and the Ants worked hard on material but still found it impossible to find work, until May when Lester quit and the revamped Ants brazened their way into the ICA Gallery restaurant, for the famous 'country and western' gig. Incidentally, Adam turned up for that in his bondage gear. For Adam was heavily under the spell of his favourite Allen Jones illustrations, and had taken to private displays wearing bondage gear for the delectation of fellow enthusiasts.

It was considered all clean fun, and just a stage further on from collecting engine numbers, stamps or contructing models of St Paul's Cathedral out of matchsticks. But when rumours of sado-masochism spread, it led to all kinds of confusion and misunderstanding. Songs like 'Deutscher Girls' did not help. Adam stood accused of being a Nazi sympathiser. It was ridiculous, but Adam was astonished and angry at the reception he began to get from critics. He became suspicious and sullen and felt he was being pilloried, ridiculed, or worse, ignored. It seemed most unfair. After all the Sex Pistols, patently unsexy, were feted and hailed as the saviours of rock, while Adam, who was better looking than any of them, was depicted as a monster.

He communicated to his small but loyal following through his own fanzine, and felt that such organs did a much better job than the recognised rock press. In its rough-typed pages he explained his philosophy of Ant music for sex people, the battle cry that was to carry him into the eighties.

He explained that sex people were not freaks to be feared, but every day, ordinary folk who enjoyed sexual practices and imagery – rather like Adam Ant. Yes – there was a sado-masochistic element in his lyrics and graphics, but this should not outrage those who campaigned for sexual equality in such sober publications as *Time Out*. These earnest campaigners had missed the point. Adam was merely battling to remove taboos which adhered to perfectly natural desires, all too often labelled as 'hang-ups'.

Adam was convinced that if such ideas could communicate in the paintings of Allen Jones and Hans Bellmer, then they could work within rock 'n' roll. Malcolm McLaren and Viv Westwood had shown the way to freedom with their shop Sex, and now Adam wanted to reach a wider public and show the kids that such imagery was harmless.

Strangely enough, when Adam's audience began to expand to reach a whole mass of very young kids, he began to cool off his use of SM imagery, in response to pressure from those who thought it might actually be harmful.

Adam was most angry at the attacks made on him in the music press which indulged in a sudden and unlikely fit of moralising. 'We've had more dirt thrown at us than a corporation dust cart,' he complained.

The trouble really began when his writing was briefly influenced by the images that had been utilised in the past by the propaganda machines of the forces of totalitarianism. Dirk might wear white sox, but he had seen one too many war films. Adam insisted however that he abhored Nazism and while his song 'Deutscher Girls' was about a member of a Nazi organisation, it was basically just an old fashioned love song. It caused a stir in Germany, not unnaturally, when the band appeared there on an early European tour. In London SM enthusiasts had scratched his back. In Germany they threatened him with guns.

Innocent Adam was taking his cue from another idol. Not Arthur Askey this time, but Lenny Bruce, the deceased American satirist, who shocked the early sixties by lifting the wraps on many a taboo subject.

In 1977 Dave Barbe joined the band, a brilliant drummer whose work gave great strength to the performances on the *White Sox* album. Lester Square had quit earlier that year just two days before the ICA gig, and was replaced by Mark Gaumont on guitar. He soon left to form his own band, and was replaced by Johnny Bivouac while Jordan came into the fold to help out with vocals. It was a powerful combination.

Adam first met Jordan in Sex when he bought his first Cambridge Rapist T-shirt. It wasn't quite Noel Coward and Vivien Leigh, but it was a touching moment. Adam invited Jordan to see him play with the band at the Man In The Moon, a pub in the Kings Road, where they were supporting X-Ray Specs with singer Polystyrene.

Jordan was most impressed by the fledgling Ant's performance and felt moved to help him. 'Jordan was like a mother to us,' said Adam. 'There was never a contract between us but she liked us and helped us a lot in the early days, when we needed help. We owed a lot to her.'

Things happened fast that year. With Jordan as manager/singer, exposure on the John Peel Show and a string of one nighters around the country, the Ant message spread.

The punk movement was to be captured on film, in *Jubilee*, directed by Derek Jarman. Adam and the Ants were invited to take part and recorded two tracks for the movie, 'Plastic Surgery' and 'Deutscher Girls'.

Adam was at the Roundhouse in Chalk Farm Road one night watching a gig by the American punk band the Ramones, when he was approached by Jarman who asked him if he'd like a bit-part in the film. Adam didn't see himself as an actor but says: 'I had no money. He offered me some, so I did it.' The film was being produced by another manager figure in Adam's life, Howard Maylan, and his appearance was built up into something more than a bit-part.

After the success of the movie, Jordan decided she had had enough of singing with the Ants and went off to Italy in search of a career in films. Jordan and Johnny Bivouac played their last gig as Ants at the Roundhouse in May 1978, once again supporting X-Ray Specs. Apart from the release of the *Jubilee* film and soundtrack album, the most important event of the year was signing a contract with Decca Records which resulted in the release of a new single, 'Young Parisians', in December 1978.

The Decca honeymoon didn't last long but the once mighty British record company signed the band for a year. There were to be two single releases and the company retained the option for an album.

There was undoubtedly an uneasy feeling at Decca that they had got sucked into the punk morass somewhat against their finer feelings. Adam realised the image they had gained through *Jubilee* and the soundtrack songs had not helped. But he felt they had a good working relationship. 'We don't have to love each other,' he thought.

'Young Parisians' came complete with saxophone and snatches or accordion in a rather camp production more suited to cabaret of theatre than the charts. The lyrics were simplistic – to say the least. 'Young Parisians are so French', warbled Adam. It was not exactly a revelation, nor was it a three-chord pogo rave up. 'I wanted it to be unpredictable,' said Adam, 'the last thing people would expect from us.'

'Lady', the B-side, was illustrated on the sleeve with a drawing of a rather tough old bird wearing a mask, boots and some species of corset. It was an amusing ditty, composed some years earlier, and inspired by a chance remark by Dave Tampin, one time drummer with the B-Sides.

The friends were at dinner when Dave

suddenly observed that he had recently seen 'a lady, and she was naked'. It seemed an ingenuous remark and caused much mirth and merriment. The song had a driving beat, urged along by the sound of a swishing cane, the anonymous caner in the studio performing with the skill born of long practice. The final, repeated phrase, 'nude, nude, nude,' recalled one of comedian Peter Cook's records on the subject of naked ladies.

With this unlikely pairing of songs, Adam was repeating history. Decca had the curious habit of recording British stars early in their careers, then dropping potential giants who were obviously working through their experimental period.

Ten years earlier, the young David Bowie had recorded strange, off the wall love songs for Decca, but had to find his feet as Ziggy Stardust with RCA.

Despite initial high hopes, Adam left Decca at the end of the year and his debut album was released on an up and coming independent label, Do-It Records. But first he gave them a single, 'Zerox', and 'Whip In My Valise', released in July 1979.

Several Decca staffers were sorry to see Adam go and felt they had missed out on a potential star artist, but the company was cutting back, and like EMI was suffering from the recession. The higher echelons of the company were not above trying to get some returns on their investment when Adam scored success elsewhere. 'Young Parisians' was reissued at the end of 1980 and this time it charted. There was a bitter sequel in 1981 when Decca tried to issue an LP of early Ant demos. Adam successfully obtained a High Court injunction against Decca Records, preventing them from using his demos.

His objections were that the recordings were not made for release, but for demonstration purposes only. They were made by a different band from the famous Ants of the eighties, they didn't represent the new band, they were of poor quality and would in any case saturate the market at a time when he had many hits in the chart.

Said Adam in a statement to the court: 'At the time when these demonstration recordings were made and I was under contract with Decca, I was not very well known. However in the last few months I have been fortunate enough to become extremely popular. Decca are now seeking to cash in on my current popularity.'

There were fourteen tracks recorded in 1978, twelve of them demos, which had already appeared on a bootleg LP. Apart from 'Young Parisians' and 'Lady' there were also 'Boil In The Bag Man', 'The Day I Met God', 'Catholic Day', 'Family Of Noise', 'Whip In My Valise', 'Fall In', 'Bathroom Function', 'Rubber People', 'Christian Dior', 'Song For Ruth Ellis', 'Red Scab' and 'Juanito The Bandito'.

The statement went on: 'I have my entire reputation to lose because they are my compositions. It's my artistic integrity at stake.'

Decca claimed that the session tapes were up to their normal standards and could be used as masters 'without the need for further recording'. They didn't think that 'one more album' could possibly harm Adam's career. But the judge thought otherwise and upheld Adam's case.

Back in August 1979 work continued apace on the debut album, the brilliant *Dirk Wears White Sox* with its title dedicated to British film actor Dirk Bogarde, star of such influential films as *Victim*, *The Servant* and *Night Porter*. The line up on the album included Dave Barbe on drums, new boy Matthew Ashman on guitar and piano, Andrew Warren on bass, and Adam on all the vocals, electric and acoustic guitar, piano and harmonica.

Bivouac had gone because he wasn't playing what Adam wanted and things just weren't working out between them. Men of vision have to make harsh decisions, and Adam did not duck them. The new guitarist was only sixteen but with his three-piece band behind him, Adam felt secure and ready for fresh battles ahead.

Chapter Four

REVOLT INTO STYLE

Towards the end of 1979 Adam met Malcolm McLaren at a party. McLaren was the man who had manipulated the media and helped build up the mythology of the Sex Pistols.

'Hello Adam. How's the Ants?' he inquired. It seemed an inconsequential remark. He didn't say, for example, 'Hello Adam, how would you like to refashion the known universe?'

But Adam was thrilled at meeting a man he regarded as a hero. They began to talk with great enthusiasm, and Adam decided that the man who had power over punk was indeed 'a great bloke'. McLaren certainly helped Adam break out of the confines of the Underground - or so it appeared. The new manager was slow to take a proper interest until Adam showed him some videos and introduced him to the Ants. It was only later that Adam began to have doubts about the wisdom of the arrangement.

He told rock writer Paulo Hewitt: 'The man, in my opinion, is a genius and he's the only genius I've ever talked to. He's a hero and heroes should be left on the wall. You should never work with them because it destroys your whole fantasy of them.'

Meanwhile Andy Warren left the band during one of its periodic upheavals, and Lee Gorman replaced him. They played what proved to be their first and last gig together at the Electric Ballroom in Camden on New Year's Day 1980. Their popularity may have been rising, but there were mutterings in the camp.

McLaren advised Adam to leave Do-It Records, and as so often happens during the perilous climb to fame, there were yet more recriminations when the record company took action after the artist had departed.

At first Adam felt qualms and twinges of guilt about quitting Do-It after they had done such a good job with 'Dirk Wears White Sox', by then showing in the independent charts. 'They were nice guys and they did a lot of good work for the Ants,' he said. But the company later put out 'Physical', Adam's anthem on which he performs his sensational strip tease, and as a B-side to boot. It was sub-standard, 'a terrible version', which had been released without his permission. It was one of his favourite songs and he was furious that

Do-It could treat it in such cavalier fashion. The trouble with making records for record companies, was they had a habit of releasing them. But this was no time to reflect on the irony of life. For worse disasters were in store.

Adam is a strong willed and determined young man and during the height of punk fever it was not unknown for the five foot two, short sighted, but karate-trained singer to attack members of the audience and even fellow musicians.

'I used to attack anybody. It was a wild, strange time,' Adam told *Sounds* in 1978. It was sado-masochistic, then it got very masochistic. At the Marquee I used to leap into the audience and let them kick me.' Adam actually had his spine dislocated by one buxom skinhead (not of his acquaintance), who thought it jolly good fun to jump up and down on his back. Adam had foolishly laid himself open to such treatment by jumping out into the audience away from the safe sanctuary of the stage. 'I got back and finished the show, but afterwards I couldn't walk.'

Sometimes at the pub gigs he would tackle members of the audience who were perhaps less than complimentary about his performance. He was vibrating with tensions and conflicts and when these spilled over into the band there were bound to be rumbles of discontent. It is not unknown for musicians to rebel against lead singers they feel are calling too many shots.

Adam had been upset at the departure of his old friend Andy Warren but there was worse in store. Adam had actually paid a considerable sum to McLaren in exchange for assistance in revamping the Ants. According to McLaren he took over the Ants and gave Adam the sack. The old band was to be re-named Bow Wow Wow and presented by McLaren to EMI as his latest post-Sex Pistols project.

McLaren had originally wanted the Ants to take part in a film about pre-teen sex which would be sold as a video. When Adam showed no interest in this dubious project, he was dismissed. When the band told Adam they were all leaving, he was shocked, but told them sternly that he was going to keep the Ants' name, if he was left with nothing else. He was high, dry and helpless, and if he felt the victim of treachery, he couldn't be blamed. He was particularly devastated at the loss of his drummer, the redoubtable Dave Barbe.

Bow Wow Wow seemed more exciting than the old Ants. They had a 14-year-old girl singer, Annabella Lu Win, backed by ex-Ants Lee Gorman, Dave Barbe and Matthew Ashman. All their releases were intended to be on tape cassettes only. They represented the next phase of punk progress. Adam belonged to yesteryear, and was doomed to obscurity - a fizzled out cult figure. Bow Wow Wow drew enormous press and media attention, and they were hailed as the true successors to the Sex

Pistols, and anybody else you cared to mention. They were launched in February 1980 on EMI and their first release was the catchily titled 'C30, C60, C90, Go' issued in July. It was not a huge success and the band were deeply disappointed they did not become instant superstars. Calling themselves Bow Wow Wow might have had something to do with it. But their gigs were probed, examined and analysed, for fear that McLaren was once again about to change the face of pop music as we knew it. Meanwhile the next revolution was being hatched in the fertile imagination of the man they said was all washed-up. To whit - one A. Ant Esq. who was supposed to have been stepped on and crushed as a mere insect, back in January.

Adam had called upon the services of an old friend, Marco Pirroni, a guitarist who had first appeared on the scene way back in 1976 with a band called the Infants.

Marco looked older than his twenty-one years, a burly figure who tended to look like one of Robin Hood's Merry Men, with a penchant for venison and good ale. In a world full of rogues and vagabonds, Marco seemed like an Honest John who would fend off attacks on Adam with a stout cudgel or at the very least, loyal rallying cries.

When Marco left the Infants to join Siouxsie and the Banshees, his old group turned into Chelsea with Gene October on vocals. The Banshees with Marco on guitar played at the 100 Club, in Oxford Street, normally a haunt associated with trad jazz. But on this occasion their performance consisted of Siouxsie and her chums screaming and shrieking their way through a version of 'The Lord's Prayer'. On drums was Sid Vicious and the gig, on September 20, 1976, went into the rock history books.

Later Marco rehearsed with Sid in a band called Flowers Of Romance, which came to nothing after Sid had thrown a glass into the audience at a gig, and was arrested.

Marco formed a band called the Beastly Cads who changed their name to the Models, and later set up Rema Rema which worked with varying success and the odd line-up change until the end of 1979.

At the beginning of 1980 he teamed up with Adam in the classic version of the Ants, with Terry Lee Miall and Merrick on drums, and Kevin Mooney on bass.

The new partnership of Marco and Adam proved singularly productive. They both needed a catalyst or pivot point to work around. They began to plot the Ants revenge on the world. While they were still with Do-It Records, the label released a single, 'Cartrouble', from the album, and the band went on the road. They were carefully watched by both CBS and Virgin Records, and eventually they signed to CBS in July 1980.

That month they released their first CBS single, 'Kings Of The Wild Frontier' coupled with 'Press Darlings' and followed up in October with 'Dog Eat Dog', both from the *Kings of the Wild Frontier* album which CBS launched on an unsuspecting world in November.

In the course of a year, Adam and Marco had brought to perfection the most exciting, palatable and commercial pop package since the great days of Glam-Rock in the early seventies. Adam had retained elements of the early Ant ideas, and refined them, developing a show that would appeal to the mass of record buyers and not just a hardcore punk following.

Adam was at pains to insist that he had done it all by himself (with the help of the Ants) and there was no Mr Big lurking in the background manipulating them.

But there were those who claimed they had assisted Adam in his rise to fame, and were not given due credit. One of those who felt a certain chagrin was Falcon Stewart, a rock group manager who displayed some of the flair of the great managers of the past like Andrew Oldham and Kit Lambert. He handled the affairs of X-Ray Specs, the band Adam had admired in the early days.

He became the Ants' manager at the beginning of 1980 and his involvement with them lasted for a year, but there was never a written contract, and he could not hold Adam when he decided to seek new management.

'Adam came to me the day that Malcolm

McLaren pinched his band,' says Falcon. 'He was very upset, of course. He had been to see me at earlier stages in his career and I had helped him with the Ants' first real gig, by putting them on as a support band to X-Ray Specs at the "Man In The Moon" and on tour. Adam was obviously incredibly talented, but I thought he had a mean streak in him.'

Falcon saw that Adam had a tight-knit following of fans but thought it was falling away rapidly and needed to be supplemented and eventually replaced by a new audience if Adam was not to sink into obscurity. It had not exactly escaped the singer's attention either.

'Adam had got fed up with being a cult figure, whose cult was disappearing. He was extremely ambitious, and one of those people who like to think they know what it's all about. But Adam had something extra and that's why I thought I could do something to help. He doesn't appreciate that now, but the things I did, when you add them up, in a subtle way, helped make it happen for him, eventually.'

Adam was reluctant to sign contracts and displayed a phobia about them probably because he had read all about the machinations of the rock business. But it didn't help foster a smooth relationship with his manager. 'We couldn't draw up accounts. It got down to silly things like that,' said Falcon, some months after the Ant breakout.

Adam told Stewart: 'I need somebody heavy to protect me.' But his manager felt this was a convenient display of paranoia, being induced as a cop-out of a tricky situation.

Said Falcon: 'Artists live a world of fantasy which can produce greatness, but it can also be very destructive. Adam does have an obsessional nature. He was prepared to go all the way for success and was quite ruthless. He took himself very seriously and became rather boring about it. That's why Kevin Mooney had to go. He was a prankster, and he was also good looking and got lots of fan letters. Marco, I felt, had nothing to do with Adam's success. He just simplified things when Adam wrote songs that were too complicated, jumbled or confused. Adam wrote everything, but Marco edited them. Marco is his side-kick, and a second opinion. Adam could have done it all by himself, but emotionally he needed someone to help him.'

Chapter Five

ANTS ON THE MARCH

Punk rock was born out of the 'situationist' movement in art, itself an off-shoot of French surrealism, which had influenced Malcolm McLaren and seduced the Kings Road wandering tribes of artists and entrepreneurs. McLaren had a record shop which gradually evolved into a place to hang out with Vivien Westwood supplying clothing for the patrons. The designs were anarchistic and intended to shock. If German propaganda posters could be revamped for modern consumption then so could all kinds of traditional images. Londoners were amazed and disturbed to see young men and girls wearing ridiculous kilts or bits of tartan and sporrans. It was visual guerrilla warfare, and a continuation of the old Yippy concept of confrontation. Old hands recalled the night when Yippies disrupted a 'live' David Frost television show, and swore in front of the cameras. The new punks were to take it all a stage further, and the Sex Pistols, perhaps unwittingly, were the standard bearers.

Indeed one of the biggest coups in the drive to shock the nation into awareness came when the Sex Pistols swore at Bill Grundy on his evening TV show and hit all the national newspapers the following day, as the press reacted in dutiful Pavlov's dog fashion. The shock tactics, outrage and over the top behaviour wasn't just an accidental outburst of yobbism, like the Rolling Stones urinating against a petrol station wall. This was the art of situationism in action.

The people caught by this upsurge were full of ideas and schemes, and seemed to fall in and out of love with each other in a confusion of emotions.

Into this vortex was sucked young Adam, the art student turned musician. Much of his subsequent charisma and, perhaps even more important, his survival traits were born out of his contact and conflict with the McLaren milieu. It was his grooming for global stardom. And when he became involved in the filming of *Jubilee* he learned about the disciplines involved, the need to get up early for filming, life on a film set, and the use of make-up. It was the theatrical and celluloid experience that he needed to help him realise his ambitions, still in the dim and distant future.

But while the experience proved useful, Adam later said of the film, 'The *Jubilee* images gave us such a lot of crap. I'm still trying to get over that. It nearly killed us. I don't regret things. If I had the choice I would not have involved the Ants. I would not have put those tracks on the album. I don't think that did us much good.'

Many saw punk rock as simply a re-run of another revolution ten years before when the Who trumpeted forth with 'My Generation' and the Rolling Stones stomped out 'Satisfaction'. It was a chance for the kids on the street to scream defiance, and shout 'We don't want you!' or 'Bother!' at the elders of the tribe. This was another burst of rock'n'roll energy.

Adam breathed that fresh, clean air of revolution, but was also witness to the other side of punk, the gay, kitsch and up-market crowd who found all shades of decadence and outrage appealing. Black plastic might have to do until real leather was affordable, but right from the beginning there was an element of cabaret about Ant performances as they played at various punk clubs. Adam was anxious not to be bracketed with the kind of music being played by U.K. Subs, then very much a cult band, who specialised in very fast three chord riffing. There had to be something more. The Ants had to be good musicians and the songs had to have something positive to say. There was no room even in the earliest Antery for mindless bellowing.

Into this vortex was sucked young Adam, student and part time musician. It all came about when he was taking the air in the Kings Road, Chelsea one afternoon, and chanced upon a curious shop midst the pubs and antiques. It was the equivalent of Winston Smith discovering the old curiosity shop in *1984* - a place of great fascination and hidden danger. The proprietors seemed to be putting into practice the erotic theory he was absorbing in his studies. Art historian Peter Webb had told him about the long tradition of eroticism in Eastern and Western art. Was this the sort of thing one might find behind locked doors in the Horniman museum?

The wealthy patrons of erotic art in the past might have found the shop run by Malcolm McLaren and Vivien Westwood somewhat tacky, with its barred windows and old rubber drawers, but Adam trembled with excitement as he tripped over the threshold, blushed, and headed for the section labelled shirts (actually fire proof caning garments). It must have spurred Adam to complete his thesis on the works of Allen Jones, although legend has it that when Ant finally met Mentor (in the Marquee Club) the latter was not entirely enamoured of his quivering protege.

But much of his subsequent charisma and perhaps even more important his survival traits were born out of his contact and conflict with this strange world. It was to be his grooming for global stardom.

While his efforts invariably met with a hostile press reception and the indifference of the industry, there were those with ears and eyes to suss what was going on, and who could sense Adam's potential. One of those in the crowd at an early gig at the Marquee in 1978 was Ian Tregoning, now a director of Do It Records.

They met and talked and eventually Ian became tour manager for the band. He also released their first album, the classic *Dirk Wears White Søx*.

'I first met Adam before he signed to Decca,' recalls Ian. 'His manager at the time reputedly sold him to Decca for £9,000. But Decca didn't have a clue what to do with him, and their A&R department was in a state of collapse. I always believed in Adam but it was a frustrating time for him when we eventually signed the group in early 1979.

'It was amazing to see how much respect he had from fans at gigs then. There was a feeling of violence at his gigs, and the audience looked frightening, but it was never as vicious as newspapers liked to make out and Adam was never really spat upon like the others in punk rock. His following then totally believed in him and what he did, and that following doesn't follow him anymore. After Decca dropped him he was still enormous as far as punks were concerned, but nobody wanted to sign him which amazed me because the A&R men were supposed to spot the tell-tale signs. Like his extraordinarily strong relationship with his fans. Punks everywhere had 'Adam & The Ants' on the backs of their leather jackets. But Adam didn't see his music developing along the three chord thrash-up lines. His maxim was 'I didn't come to cater for an audience, I came to create one.'

Ian went out on tour with the band during their major outing of 1979. He could closely observe what was happening in the Ant ranks at this crucial time. 'Adam said he was unhappy with the musicianship of the band and he didn't want the old 1-2-3-go thrash-ups anymore. He wanted the music to be more sophisticated. But he was very close to the drummer Dave Barbe, and they had known each other for years. Malcolm McLaren claimed he gave Adam ideas about using percussion, but Dave and Adam had already used syn drums for things like heavy hand-claps.'

As Adam emphasised later: 'Adam and the Ants are not a punk band. We've moved on from that. I went through countless phases until I knew what my look should be. That's why I have great respect for anyone who can develop their own style. I firmly believe in entertaining people. We are living in austere times. Everywhere you look there is hardship and unemployment. I want to take people's minds off things like that when they come to my shows. The people who come to our gigs get a kick out of looking good and dressing up. We wanted to create an electrifying atmosphere, so that the kids left soaked in sweat and exhausted. We put tremendous emphasis on drums and voices in the music because they are so provocative. I was inspired by hearing the chants of the Burundi tribe of Africa. They played a very exciting form of music and it showed me a direction as far away from rock'n'roll as possible.'

But before the influence of the African drummers could penetrate deep into the Ant psyche, there were more problems to be solved, and aggravation sorted out.

Adam decided to work with Do It Records at the start of 1979 and, says Ian Tregoning: 'When Adam was with us there was a lot of debate going on during the mixing of *Dirk Wears White Søx*. There were a couple of songs he recorded – "Kick" and "Physical" which he didn't put on the album in case they sounded too much like heavy metal.

'It was a time of great flux, as Adam's ideas began to gel. It took a couple of months for us to realise which way he was developing. During the mixing stages he decided to split up the band. The album however was made during August and September 1979 and released on November 30, 1979.

'I think it was a mistake when Adam dropped Matthew Ashman because he was a very good guitarist. But in August 1979 Adam wanted Marco to join them. But Andy Warren's girl friend Max (real name Dorothy) was on drums with Marco in Rema Rema, and if Adam had pinched their guitarist it would have broken up the group.'

It was only after the Bow Wow Wow-Malcolm McLaren debacle in January 1980 that the way was clear to obtain the services of Marco in seemly fashion, and in any case Rema Rema was in the throes of disintegration. In the new Ants, Terry Lee Miall, on drums, came in from The Models, where he was known as Terry Day, and had worked alongside Marco Pirroni. The other Ant drummer, known to all as Merrick, was in fact producer Chris Hughes, who was to produce *Kings of The Wild Frontier*.

During their year together Ian Tregoning thought that Adam displayed considerable suspicion about independent labels in general. His defence mechanism worked overtime.

'It was because he was ignored when he started, and he was also wary about whether royalties were being paid,' says Ian. 'But we were very straight with him in our dealings. A lot of chaos tends to surround Adam because he tends to hop from one idea to another very quickly!'

A major dispute occurred between Adam and Do It over the problem of the release of a version of 'Physical'.

'What happened was that 14 tracks were recorded for *Dirk Wears White Søx*. Eleven were used and three were not. The other three tracks were recorded but unmixed. I tracked down Chris Hughes and asked him to do a remix. Adam heard about what we were doing and thought it was a good idea. McLaren had just taken his band and he wanted to hit back by making a sudden reappearance. So we planned a four track EP with 'Cartrouble', 'Kick', 'Physical' and 'Friendship'. We did it, then Adam said he wanted it scrapped because it was just a guide vocal. We thought that was bullshit because it was good quality.'

Eventually Do It put 'Physical' out as a secret B-side on the single release featuring 'Zerox' in a limited 3000-copy run. There was no advertising, but the whole pressing sold out in three days, as fans quickly sussed that 'Whip In My Valise' – the official B-side – had been substituted with 'Physical'.

Despite the secrecy, it caused friction between Adam and Do It. 'He was annoyed about it because he thought he could do a better version with Marco on guitar. Our one was done with the old band. His one is now a B-side on 'Dog Eat Dog' (CBS). He made a comment about us to let off steam on the record, but I thought it was rather petty.'

It is remarkable that Adam has maintained his sunny and cheerful disposition, apart from the occasional outburst, because as Ian says: 'He got an indescribably bad press. There were articles in music papers that were ridiculous. They either called him a fascist or a wanker, or else they ignored him. *Melody Maker* were quite fair and there was a girl on *Sounds* called Jane Suck who gave him really great reviews early on.'

'Because of the bad press we decided just to concentrate on the things that mattered, playing gigs and making records. The problem was caused by "Deutscher Girls". The press hated him for writing that. But they didn't realise he had a tremendous sense of humour. He has written a lot of very clever songs. But the press thought he was being pernicious. They took his use of swastika imagery literally and were being very po-faced.'

It is hardly surprising that the swastika symbol should create an uproar. To a previous generation it signified terror and caused revulsion. To a poorly-educated new generation, in their innocence and ignorance, they took a child-like glee in confronting the survivors of Nazism with images of the past.

Says Ian: 'The early punks were interested in the swastika as a symbol because they got such a strong reaction, and a lot of art students were interested in the imagery too. Adam was not into politics at all.'

Even so, there were many who could not forgive this academic interest by innocents in the recent past. And it rubbd off on Adam.

'There was one review of *Dirk Wears White Søx* that was just puerile garbage,' recalls Ian. 'It didn't even qualify as garbage. It was just very fashionable to hate the band. Nick Kent wrote one article about them that inspired Adam to write "Press Darlings" which was on

the B-side of "Kings Of The Wild Frontier".
Adam was very upset about the criticism. He
felt that one article could reach 200,000 people
and he needed to catch up and put the picture
right. He suffered the most absurd abuse so he
wrote a very funny article in a fanzine about it.
The critics were intimidated by something
they hadn't created. Newspapers like to think
they create the artists and Adam went totally
against that concept. That's why he wasn't
accepted by the media.'

'He was thrashing around in the wilderness
for three years trying to get his music
accepted, but on his own terms. No one has
really understood what he was trying to do.
Now of course he is very successful with the
young girls . . .'

Like many of Adam's early supporters Ian
Tregoning has experienced a certain disen-
chantment with what he sees as the decline of
the Ant experience.

'I'm not impressed by half the songs on
Kings Of The Wild Frontier and "Stand And
Deliver" was rubbish. I think Adam, some-
where along the line, has sidetracked himself.'

But Adam himself answered such criticism
by saying, 'I was never involved in the no-
heroes idea, and I was not interested in
anarchy of any kind – except sexual anarchy.
On *Dirk Wears White Søx* I dealt with quite
heavy sexual taboos like leather fetishism and
transvestism – subjects which fascinated me

sincerely because I feel there's some kind of beauty involved.

'I think Bowie helped sell the idea that it wasn't evil or decadent for a man to wear make-up or present himself in a feminine way. I think a lot of pain is caused by people being intimidated by their sexual desires. I don't think there should be any intimidation toward any sexual community no matter what it is.'

He explained that a complete cross section of kids were attracted to his creation. 'I've seen punks dancing with skinheads, trendies and rock'n'rollers,' he said with awe. 'We're not just aiming at punks, anyone can be seduced by our music. I just want kids to be positive and celebrate their youth, dress up and have a good time.'

There is a simplistic purity about Adam's idealism undoubtedly born out of his earlier experiences which seemed to heighten his powers of concentration and dedication. It is interesting to note that nearly all the great religious leaders of the past experienced their initial revelation whilst undergoing extreme hardship, on rocky roads covering great distances, or whilst lost on mountain tops or in some barren wilderness. The deprivation and hardship undoubtedly cleared their minds for the task ahead. Something similar must have happened to Adam, lost in the wilderness of pre-1980, assailed by robbers and pelted with the stones of the philistines.

During his long struggle against the powers of darkness, Adam drew up a manifesto which explained the Ants were working and performing for a future age! 'We are optimists and reject the Blank Generation ideal. We are interested in music, entertainment, action and excitement, anything young and new.' As a rallying cry it was enough to bring strong men to tears and masses to toss their hats in the air and shout 'Huzzah!' Without such idealism mankind is doomed. And the cold facts, all rhetoric aside, are that Stuart Goddard did actually achieve all he set out to do, and with stunning rapidity. When success came, Adam magnanimously claimed victory, not for himself, but for his fans. 'It's nice for them to be proven right. I wanted success. "Cult" was just a safe word for "loser",' he vowed.

Chapter Six

ADAM TALKING

The Autumn of 1980 will forever live in the memory of Adam Ant and all his myriad friends and supporters. It saw the birth of a bright new star, whose arrival brought good cheer and old fashioned pop enthusiasm back to a scene otherwise groaning with despair, gloom and despondency.

With unemployment rising fast, inflation eroding the value of what money could be earned, racial tension and youthful violence boiling over, and the effects of recession biting into every imaginable industry, including the business of making pop music, the nation was in need of a tonic, some form of distraction that was appealing to men, women, children, yea and even the halt and lame, as they gazed at their TV screens filled with news of fresh disasters.

For those being made redundant or joining

the dole queues for the first time, the arrival of Adam with painted face, tribal rhythms, and stream of hits brought back some of the carefree innocence of the sixties, when England was swinging, which they may have read about or experienced at first hand.

Industrialists, about to shoot themselves at the sight of downward spiralling sales graphs, lowered their revolvers and found their mouths contorting into unaccustomed smiles, and they reached for the intercom.

'Miss Perkins, what is that strange noise emitting from your wireless receiver?'

'Why Sir, don't you know? 'Tis Adam & The Ants, a fine new beat group, they do say. Me and my Jack go a jiving to his music regularly like at the Village 'All.'

'Really Miss Perkins, there is no need to adopt that irritating West Country accent. I happen to know you come from Catford. But Adam Ant you say. And his Ants?'

'Yes Sir, they be sweeping the nation with their new sound, and all their records are in the hit parade. I have purchased several of his discs myself, and even own a long playing microgroove record called *Kings Of The Wild Frontier* which they do say has caused some concern among ethnic minorities in the North Americas.'

'Never mind that, Perkins. If we start selling Adam Ant T-shirts instead of galvanised zinc spectroscopes, I think we can save this old company of ours and a thousand jobs. Perkins *]* get me the warehouse.'

Ant Fever cut across all barriers of class and occupation during October as 'Dog Eat Dog' began its swift climb up the charts, helped by a vitally important appearance on BBC TV's *Top Of The Pops* on the 16th of the month.

'Antmusic', from the album, was re-mixed as a single and that entered the chart in December, while 'Dog Eat Dog' blasted its way into the Top Five.

After all the years of struggle and panic, Adam felt an icy calmness, and a quiver of excitement, as he realised he had lift-off and the great gamble was going to work.

When he recorded *Kings Of The Wild Frontier* it was all the Ants had left. They had financed their own tours to promote the new music and it was make or break time.

The buzz that Adam had finally cracked it seemed to sweep around the media like wildfire. Perhaps one of his greatest assets at that crucial time was his own ability to talk lucidly and intelligently about his aims and his music. This was no ranting demagogue, no leering lout, but a man with charm, obvious sincerity and considerable talent.

And for once, here was a pop artist who had encouraging, optimistic ideas about the state of rock. He was an idol who readily announced his dislike of the trend towards violence that was already spilling over from the football terraces into pop clubs and venues, before it was noticed by the national press and eventually took the form of tragic riots. Adam thought it was important that young people took pride in themselves and sought creative ways to find enjoyment. He had seen the nihilism of punk and its effects over a long period at close quarters, and he was one of the few who could speak up from a position of experience and authority.

His mixture of tribal rock and sex appeal was both refreshing and posed no threat to society. And surprisingly he was made welcome even by the most pitiless of rock pundits who might have been expected to put Adam among the wets and non-combatants.

Adam, clad in baggy trousers and an old raincoat, his effective disguise against being spotted on the streets and mobbed, talked with great lucidity and flashes of humour as we sat in the CBS record company office.

When it was suggested he'd become a star of the first magnitude in 1981, he looked embarrassed and concerned.

'I'm trying to act as cool as I can, but inside I've got a strange feeling of nerves,' said Adam. 'It was all down to being in the right place at the right time. I was thrilled at the success for the writing team of myself and Marco because that's been very important. I just needed that other train of thought, relaxation and discipline that Marco has. We have totally different ideas and styles. In the studio Marco really helps because he is a totally studio-orientated person.'

'I'm awful in the studio – terribly impatient. So working with Marco has been great for us both. We work as a team. We decided it was either going to be a Rodgers & Hammerstein set up, or forget it!'

'The music we are hitting on now is the most satisfying for me to date although I wouldn't say that anything I've done before was put out with any less degree of commitment. The influences on Marco and myself are very diverse but have a kind of filmic quality. We like John Barry and Link Wray.'

John Barry was the British-born composer and arranger who had such a big influence on the rock scene in the late fifties. He wrote the backing for Adam Faith's early records and also wrote the theme tunes for TV shows like *Juke Box Jury* as well as the James Bond movie theme. Link Wray was the part Shawnee Indian rocker who recorded the classic 'Rumble' in 1958 and enjoyed a come back in interest in 1971. Traces of their work are evident in the wide screen approach that permeat *Kings* but Adam was being too modest when he later claimed that he had no original ideas of his own. There may have been examples to inspire him from the past, but that goes for practically every performer in every field.

Adam agrees that vocally he has not been influenced by any Western performers. 'Instead, for the last two years I've collected

French imported albums of tribal music. They're expensive and hard to get, but I bought one of Pygmy music and albums by Aborigines whose music appeals to me on a structural level.

'They use chants, grunts and voices that come in all over the place!'

This influence was most notable, of course, on the Ants' remarkable composition 'Dog Eat Dog' which began with a powerful drum beat that increased in volume while Adam sang unexpected whoops and cries which sounded almost comic on first hearing, until the significance of it all filtered in.

Adam had listened a lot to Cream as a kid and admired the drumming of Ginger Baker who also has affinities for African, tribal music.

'It was difficult to achieve that effect on a singles level because the Western ear will ignore certain things,' says Adam. 'We had to exaggerate certain rhythmic and structural things and make them very simple. The follow up single "Antmusic" had everything on it, from a structural point of view, that I wanted to put on future LPs. We used a whole range of instruments on it that were virtually home made to get the right effects.'

The tracks were all recorded at Rockfield in Monmouth and the album was produced by Chris Hughes.

'The most important thing for us was to get a SOUND. We threw out a lot of good songs that were quite exciting, just so that we could go for the right sound. We started writing all the new songs with that sound in mind and it was the hardest thing to do.'

A solid, recognisable and distinctive sound had been the cornerstone of much classic pop before Adam & The Ants. The Beatles had it, and so did Phil Spector, the Carpenters, Abba, the legendary Link Wray and of course The Shadows. Adam thinks there are fewer people who can claim an original sound than have hit records.

'We spent three years arriving at our sound, and we had to be very brutal with our own work to get it. It drove us mad being in the country when we recorded the album because we are not country people. We had to use planks of wood on "Antmusic" to get the sound we wanted, and we had to work out every beat. The same went for "Kings Of The Wild Frontier" (title track). We used two drummers because there was no way we could achieve that sound "live" without them.'

In Autumn 1980 Adam took the concert halls of Old England by storm and again considerable thought went into the package they were presenting their fans. The Ants were determined to give value for money and a show that not only entertained but helped, by subtle means, to spread positive thoughts among the young, to counteract what the wise young Ant could already see was infecting the hearts and minds of British youth. 'It was showbiz, but not just glam and glitter.'

Adam had already gained a remarkable following and the single 'Kings' quickly sold 40,000 without any problem. 'I had obviously accumulated 40,000 fans over the years,' says Adam, in defiance of those who had claimed his cult status had been slipping. 'When we did *Top Of The Pops* on TV, it sold over 100,000, which was great! People say the record business is slumping, but I don't see anything wrong with it. The trouble is, while there are many new groups out there – and they send me their tapes – they have naïve charm all right, but they are not commercially viable. That sort of thing comes with time, and getting the right format. You can't do it by magic. You can have a heavy producer come in or a top manager, but they don't guarantee success.

Adam denied that he had anybody manipulating his career and his success, while he was aware that many were trying to claim some modicum of credit. 'No, its always been a clandestine thing. I've kept a very close rein on all the promotional stuff, and while the packaging looks slick, it's all been done by the band and designed by myself.'

In recent years, packaging and merchandising have become increasingly important to the rock business. Some of the big rock shows at venues like Earls Court and Wembley began to look like Eastern Bazaars with their plethora of stands selling everything from hot dogs to T-shirts, badges, jeans, jackets, shirts, and posters. Some despise and disparage such commercialisation especially when it reaches the stage of kids being offered Peter Frampton gold watches or Elvis Presley Cadillacs. But Adam thinks that design and packaging are important and perfectly valid adjuncts to the whole pop process. Either we have pop music and accept all its offshoots, or else we ban all such activities and spend our time in contemplation and prayer (not a bad idea at that).

'Packaging plays a very close number three to the music,' says Adam. 'For the Ants, Roxy Music were the example of a band who set a style and consistency. Marco and I have written top ten records and we don't want to go back now. At the same time we still want to be relaxed and have fun.'

Was Adam in danger of being hoist by his own petard, if he didn't mind me bringing his petard into the conversation?

'I dunno,' he said, hunching still further into his raincoat and allowing a blond curl, midst a sea of black hair to fall over his forehead. 'We are not interested in just being a singles band. We want every song to be a classic, and also, the way the kids are feeling now because of the recession, we want to give them some "up" music, something that is rich and has a wild nobility.'

There wasn't much opportunity for the average petrol pump operative to adopt the trappings of a noble savage, even if Adam could do it for them.

'That's true,' said Adam, 'but look through and beyond the trappings. As soon as you say "warrior" you think of violence, but that's not the case. When I listened to the records of the tribes, hammering their bits of wood together, I felt a bit of a hypocrite, a white boy copping the tribal rhythms. There was nothing new in that. So I read a lot of books too, about the Zulu people and the Masai warriors, and of course the American Indians. "Dog Eat Dog" was very Zulu. You'll notice that heavy beat in the middle of the song? We had to hit drum cases about thirty times to get that sound!

'And that's styled on Zulu warriors hitting their shields. The reason why I've used the warrior theme is because warriors are like peacocks. They have integrity and independence.

'In their appearance they use a unique make-up which sets them aside from everybody else in the tribe. They are ABOVE violence. And I think violence is a very unfortunate and brutal thing that is creeping into music. The football terraces are moving into the concert hall.'

Adam is aware of his role at the head of the heap of groups who fought their way out of the club scene, and he is keen to see his fellow musicians help restore a scene that at one time seemed in real danger of sinking into irreversible decline. 'I think the situation now demands more effort from bands,' says Adam. 'I think the kids are sick of green vinyl. They want good records and a good show. On our tours we are aware we have a very young audience. They tend to start from twelve upwards and loads of them write to me. I was getting sixty letters a week.' (Adam gets many more now, with a backlog of twenty sacks of mail considered about average.)

'I tried to write to them all personally and from that I knew exactly what was happening.' In the end it got too much, and Adam couldn't hope to answer every single one himself. 'A lot of the kids told me they couldn't get in to see their favourite bands. I think that's bad. There should be more opportunities for the younger ones to see bands, and I don't think there is a teenybop market as such anymore. Kids are far more tuned into what their big brothers listen to.'

Adam set out to play shows that the younger kids could attend at convenient hours. And he also declared war on deejays who supplied the in-between music at rock shows and assumed they knew the tastes of their audience. 'They tend to put out the music THEY like. When we were booked in during the early days, they'd say "Ah, punk band." So they'd stick on Cockney Rejects and the Angelic Upstarts and I can't STAND all those aggro and oi bands - the boot boys. I think they encourage violence. When a kid goes to his first gig he is bound to get taken in by the whole event and what's going down.'

Adam counteracted the doctrine of violence long before it was exposed in the national press.

That led to the setting up of the Ant Disco. Each Ant was invited to go into a studio for a day and record his own choice of music and then act as a bona fide Ant DJ. Their choice ranged from Dolly Parton to Marc Bolan. Adam has a big thing about the late and much loved star of Glam Rock. He admits without shame that he once asked Marc for his autograph and sent a fan letter to Bryan Ferry. He pinned the answer on his bedroom wall.

Long before most of the press discovered what was happening beneath their noses, the Ant people were on the march during the months leading up to chart take-off time.

They were his hard core of fans and, recalled Adam: 'One thing they picked up on was oil painting. Remember how American air pilots painted "Lucky Lady" on the backs of their flying jackets? Well the Ant people had beautiful paintings on their jackets and the most amazing tattoos. That's when they started coming to the gigs, specially dressed up.'

Adam was famous for his tatttoo. He has, as every Ant fan worth his formic acid knows, 'Pure Sex' emblazoned on his forearm. His secret wife, Eve, later revealed that he has another tattoo which caused him to faint when it was cut into his body with a razor blade. Hardly surprising, and it's not the sort of practice to be recommended to even the oldest and least impressionable Ant fan. Was it a good thing that pop stars should become leaders of youth cults? Didn't they invariably do more harm than good?

'It happens anyway and I think you do have to be careful not to preach. When a fan comes up to me wearing all the make-up, I'm as nervous as he is, and as flattered. To me it's a great compliment for someone to ask for an autograph.'

'I suppose I am in a great position at concerts to talk a lot and make speeches, which I don't do. I just want to learn a lot of jokes, because the whole thing is supposed to be fun! But it's hard to tell jokes on stage when your heart is pounding and your throat is drying up.'

So Adam has no policies and no politics? 'None at all.'

Adam was adamant that he would not follow the path taken by another cult hero, Jimmy Pursey, a while back, which led to a tragic chain reaction. 'I've never really met Jimmy Pursey but I remember him down the Vortex promoting a kind of skinhead revival. Because there were no skinheads in '77 at all. Then it got promoted and it grew and I could see it happening. You reap what you sow. What's a kid gonna do if you tell him, "You've got nothing, you've got no hope." There's gonna be anger isn't there? With our group we just try to present Ant music for sex people. Everybody likes sex and I hope everybody will like Ants! My message is all in the title track of *Kings Of The Wild Frontier*.'

Adam was keen to emphasise the importance of the live show in the future and is not convinced by the technologists who tell us that we shall spend all our days locked in at home watching an endless stream of flickering images on the telescreens.

'The video disc will come and go!' he insists. 'There are two factors I shall be guided by in the future. The video disc *will* come and go much faster than people imagine and the only thing that will be left will be the LIVE show. And in the eighties, the big show will be the thing. And it's going to be more for the family, like American football is more for the family.'

Adam refuses to accept the principle that the music business is like a boxing ring with the contestants slugging it out for superiority. He prefers to think of it as a coal mine with each performer carving out his own niche (or nuggets).

'Dexy's Midnight Runners and Madness, for example, do their shows and enjoy themselves, but they are not competing within the framework of the coalmine. There's plenty of room for everybody and there's no need for a sense of competition. The Ants started with five fans. The same five still come to see us, but hopefully there are 100,000 more now.'

How was Ant music created and knocked into shape? Adam carries a diary around with him and he jots down ideas as he travels about the place, from a yodel to a complete set of lyrics. He firmly believes in starting a song with a strong title.

'The title will set me off thinking about the lyrics and then I have to make sure the syllables are right. If you cram in too many words, you have to catch your breath while singing them. We're quite old fashioned on one level. I had the whole band tutored for singing lessons by Tona DeBrett. She's very good. She was introduced to me by Malcolm McLaren. She tried to teach Johnny Rotten to sing. He took her a Doors album and said he wanted to sing like Jim Morrison! She's helped me a lot. Physically there is no way I could get through an hour and thirty minutes of Ant music, and move, and entertain without using her techniques. We tape every show by the way. And it's horrible hearing all those bum notes!

'When we were recording the album I was bent right over, holding my rib cage, and I jumped up and down.'

This seemed a rather bizarre practice but I was sure there was some rational explanation, forthcoming.

Sure enough Adam revealed all. 'It's a way

to get adrenalin flowing. I couldn't just stand there and do a cabaret number. You have to get your diaphragm working well, or else you can do your throat in after one night. We all do exercises before we go on, pushing up and breathing out and panting.'

Adam exposed his diaphragm and gave me a brief demonstration involving various strangled cries and stretching limbs. 'It looks RIDICULOUS,' he admits.

All this explains and demonstrates how seriously Adam took his attack on stardom. But he told me: 'I find it totally embarrassing even to discuss stardom and how I might cope with it. I just want to make sure that every record I put out has quality from the cover to the music. And we want to make music that appeals to everybody, whatever their age. I want our music to be properly arranged. Not many people know this, but the Sex Pistols' album was very heavily arranged. The art of arranging is not given much credit these days. We want to arrange our music down to the last second!'

Chapter Seven

'THE MAGNIFICENT FIVE'

~~What strange~~ge response did Adam Ant trigger in the public consciousness at the end of 1980? What caused such a wave of unrest? It was like the excitement engendered by greeting a beautiful stranger, stepping out of his war canoe onto the sandy shores of our mind. What strange gifts did he bring? Who were these other chaps? Why, whither and whence were the questions that sprang to our lips as we jostled around, feeling the travellers' brightly coloured clothing, offering beads and trinkets and attempting to communicate in their strange tongue.

'You *Ant* people?'

'Ugh. We are wild nobility. New Royal Family. We play sex music for Ant people. You fetch money. Buy tickets for pow wow. Heap big tour coming to town. Avoid unauthorised rip offs. See my manager.'

The impact of the Ants was total because they emerged armed with a mystique, a story to tell and a lot of songs that all proved to have hit potential. It was all too easy to draw parallels. To some they seemed like a young, hipper and prettier Village People. Others could hear overtones of Cliff and the Shadows, and eventually Adam himself cheerfully acknowledged that he hadn't any original ideas to offer. But he was being modest. The Ants concept ("A whole package" as the Village People would say) was decidedly fresh and innovative. It was a team effort with Adam at the helm.

It seemed incredible that Adam and Marco could have got such a hit formula together in the space of six months, but they had the impetus of the Bow Wow Wow episode behind them acting as a spur. Combined with all their artistic influences, rough and tough experience at the hands of sado-masochists and rock critics, and a boiling desire to succeed, the result was a veritable Ant explosion, triggered by the release of their first CBS single 'Kings Of The Wild Frontier' in summer 1980.

The buzz about Adam seemed to spread around the media with amazing speed and by the Autumn he was being interviewed and feted almost hourly. In the meantime rehearsals for the major tour went ahead and the band made its first appearance on BBC TVs *Top Of The Pops*. They performed 'Dog Eat

Dog' and the result was a top ten hit, and within weeks the band's second album *Kings Of The Wild Frontier* shot up to the top of the charts where it stayed for over eight months. Their third single, 'Antmusic', also from the album was only prevented from reaching number one by the reissue of John Lennon's classic 'Imagine', which mourned his murder in New York in December.

'Antmusic' was remixed as a single at the Matrix Studios, a tiny hideaway near the British Museum, while 'Dog Eat Dog' was already marching up the chart. It was the same month, in October, that Adam achieved the transition from cult hero to unashamed pop star. The Ants went to BBC TV's Lime Grove studios for *Top Of The Pops* and met, in passing, the Prime Minister, Margaret Thatcher, who had been on an official visit to the BBC.

The pop establishment began to rave about the new Ant sound and Adam was particularly delighted that his old hero Bryan Ferry expressed highly favourable comments about the 'Antmusic' single on BBC Radio's *Roundtable* discussion show.

On November 9, 1980 the band began its first tour of major venues, opening at the Royal Court Theatre, Liverpool. By the time they got to Glasgow the *Kings Of The Wild Frontier* LP had got to number four and there was much cause for celebration. But there was one cause for alarm when the band played at

Hull College and the building caught fire and had to be evacuated. The band ploughed on, playing at such venues as West Runton Pavilion, the Top Rank, Sheffield, St George's Hall, Blackburn and Leeds Polytechnic. Adam had wanted to play matinees for kids, but complained that at that stage the promoters hadn't realised his pulling power and status.

By December Ant videos were flooding the airwaves and 'Dog Eat Dog' was number four in the chart, hotly pursued by 'Antmusic'. Adam held a press conference for his favourite kind of press, the fanzines, and also appeared on *Roundtable* himself. He was to receive also the ultimate acolade, a pie in the face on ITV's *Tiswas*, and his appeal for a nation of pop-hungry children was confirmed by appearances on *Multi Coloured Swap Shop*, which somehow seemed more relevant than *The Old Grey Whistle Test*, which was also honoured by a visit.

January 1981 was a crazy month. Adam flew to New York for his first promotional visit and was being interviewed non-stop, with phone calls back home and to Australia, where the Ants were already a hit on such local TV shows as the celebrated *Countdown*.

Ant music dominated the chart, as a horde of new fans caught up with his output and laid their hands on anything bearing his logo. *Kings Of The Wild Frontier* was the number one album and eventually went Double

Platinum, selling in excess of 750,000. At the same time 'Antmusic' was the number two single, while older records 'Zerox', 'Car Trouble' and even the ancient Decca recording 'Young Parisians' from 1978 became hits.

In February the band took a controversial step by consenting to appear at the London Palladium for the Royal Children's Variety Performance in aid of the NSPCC. They played 'Antmusic' and after the show Adam met Princess Margaret. It was after this that bassist Kevin Mooney left the group, claiming that the Ants were heading towards the kind of megastardom that was a million miles away from the stews of the rock 'n' roll experience. But there was no stopping the Ants now. Said the Princess: 'Please give me your autograph.' Adam obliged.

On February 9 the band recorded their next single, 'Stand And Deliver', at London's Townhouse Studios. Already there were mutterings that Adam's incredible run of luck must be over, that his appeal was on the wane and that he was bound to catch a cold and flop miserably. It was going to be like Bill Haley & The Comets all over again - too many hits in too short a space of time. Indeed there were worries about over exposure within the Ant camp, which made the crushing of Decca's plans to reissue their album of early demos all the more vital.

Adam needed all his reserves of energy to cope with the demands on his time. There were photo sessions, more radio, TV and press interviews and odd spots like his appearance on Jimmy Savile's show *Jim'll Fix It*. This was rather a touching episode. A young viewer, 10-year-old Gary Blackwood, had written to the BBC saying that he loved playing the drums and his biggest ambition was to sit in with the Ants. This was duly arranged and Gary played drums alongside Terry Lee Miall and Merrick. At the end of the show, Adam presented the bemused Gary with a snare drum.

While 'Antmusic' went to number one in Australia, Adam began work on making the 'Stand And Deliver' video with TV producer Mike Mansfield, which was to create a sensational new wave of Ant activity.

'Stand And Deliver' eventually went to number one after its release on May 1, and confounded all those who had predicted an early Ant demise. The combination of video and record had been devastating, as once more Adam came up with a new look, this time his highwayman's garb. In fact Adam was at pains to deny that his 'Stand And Deliver' image was simply a new gimmick.

'We're not going from anything to anything else,' he told critics in April. 'We're just going to incorporate everything I've done. This look is the combination of four different make-ups I've developed over the past few years. But I'm always trying to think ahead.'

Fans were fascinated by Adam's clothes and

bombarded him with requests for information about where he got them, so they could improve their own attempts to dress up.

Adam had to explain to his adoring fans: 'Image is such a meaningless word. I don't have to dress up. I like smart clothes and leather. I do all my own make-up, using everything from Clockwork Orange, traditional 'English, Japanese Kabouki and Red Indian influences. But it has to be co-ordinated and my friend Dave Whitney helps me in that department. We hire the clothes and we can't buy them because many of them are antiques. The make-up mostly comes from Marks & Spencer.'

Fans were most intrigued by his military jacket and he told them: 'You can't buy a jacket like it because it is very special and rare. It was the one actually worn by David Hemmings when he played the part of an officer in the film *Charge Of The Light Brigade*.'

The vexed question of clothes reached a peak when his secret wife Eve who had been working for him as a designer clamoured for attention and recognition in a series of national newspaper articles. Adam tended to tell people simply that: 'A girl called Eve makes the band's shirts. She's just graduated from St. Martin's College of Art.'

Eve was still working on the stage clothes for the band's projected world tour when the article appeared in the *Sunday People* in July, revealing their marriage and complaining she had not received any money from Adam beyond her wages as the group's designer. Shortly after they appeared Eve was sacked from the band and Adam was said to be upset and hurt by her action in seeking publicity.

Eve had once worked as a rock musician in a band called Tralalah, when she was living in a Battersea warehouse with singer Toyah Wilcox. Toyah and Adam rowed as both were such strong personalities and also suspected each other of ripping off ideas. 'I don't like Adam much,' said Toyah recently. 'And when we met at *Top Of The Pops*, we didn't speak to each other.'

The row came while *Jubilee* was being made. Eve told reporters: 'When Adam came to visit me at the warehouse, the atmosphere became very icy and they didn't talk. Adam thought Toyah was trying to copy him.'

Another explanation for the sudden disappearance of Kevin Mooney from the band, was not so much the Ants' appearances before royalty, but the fact that Eve Goddard had lived with Kevin for a while. She it was who introduced him to Adam who took him into the group. Said Eve: 'I used to go to gigs and see my husband and my boyfriend on the same stage. I wanted them both to do well.' When Eve and Kevin split up, she claimed that Adam actually fired him from the band.

Eve planned to set up her own clothes designing and knitwear business and also threatened to create a new look 'for another band'. The Empire of the Ants seemed to be clamouring for independence, at least in the outer colonies!

Such human reactions were inevitable. As soon as success rears its head, and especially when it comes at such speed, there is bound to be a whiff of jealousy in the air and a human characteristic is to topple the giants of any field, usually by attacking at the weakest point.

But if Adam came under fire, then he showed no signs of wavering in his determined onslaught. When 'Stand And Deliver' was announced, Joe Strummer of the Clash grunted, somewhat ungraciously: 'What's he doing now – The Milkman?' Adam found this most amusing and congratulated Mr Strummer on his sense of humour. Adam could, after all, laugh all the way to the Building Society.

Adam announced that he was pleased with both his lyrics and the sound that had captured the hearts and minds of so many fans. The single was from their next album and it would surprise everyone with its new direction. He thought the video with 'Stand And Deliver' was very important.

'The lyrics were about not being intimidated by any particular fashion. The video was an Erroll Flynn epic – with us doing all the things I like seeing in Hollywood movies in three minutes.'

The video showed Adam holding up an eighteenth-century carriage and jumping through a mullioned window into a dinner party, much to the alarm of the guests. 'I endangered my life making that film – there was no way I could fake it.'

Mike Mansfield who made the video with his own production company had created the legendary pop show *Supersonic* at London Weekend TV during the mid-seventies.

Says Mike: 'Visually Adam is the most aware pop star I have ever worked with. He's a very visual performer and is totally aware of the function and potential of video. A lot of people make records but have no stage appeal. Adam is made for video and has wonderful ideas. He has Hollywood in his head and he has enormous charisma, with a high degree of acting ability which is totally instinctive. He can tell a story with his eyes, and when he sings a song, he acts out the story. It adds another dimension to his performance.

'When we work together on a video he comes to me with his ideas, usually on scraps of paper and in notebooks. We work our way through them and I put them into practice. It worked very well on "Stand And Deliver" and I like to think it helped keep him at number one for five weeks.

'Adam has unlimited enthusiasm which has grown rather than been swamped by success. In his case success breeds success and he is in control of everything. His training as a graphic artist has helped him a lot. He will become a modern-day Valentino. He has an amazingly photogenic face.'

Mike revealed that when Adam went crashing through the glass during "Stand And Deliver" there was an added problem apart from plucking up the courage to make the jump.

'The glass we used was opaque. He couldn't see through it and had to jump blind, while we held the cameras down low. He takes direction very well!'

Chapter Eight

ANT MUSIC

1977 was the year of the *Star Wars* theme, of hits by The Jam, Tom Robinson, the Muppets and Abba. It was the year of 'Mull Of Kintyre' and *Never Mind The Bollocks — Here's the Sex Pistols*. It would take a brave man to seek any discernible social significance in this random fluctuation in public tastes.

But what became obvious was a hammering at the gates of the pop music establishment by the new forces of rebellion. It was also the year of the Derek Jarman film *Jubilee*, made to celebrate the punk rock movement, its title a kind of satirical poke at the national celebrations for the Queen's jubilee year. Whatever the merits of the film, it helped launch Adam Ant's recording career, for he contributed his two penn'orth in the shape of the tracks 'Deutscher Girls' and 'Plastic Surgery', the former track causing Adam endless trouble in later years.

Both tracks were released on the Polydor soundtrack album from the film, but Adam and the Ants' debut single came with the release in 1978 of 'Young Parisians' in a black and white picture sleeve. It was the kind of performance that could have wrecked his reputation for ever among those who like their rock music beefy and predictable. For this was a million miles away from punk or any other kind of rock.

An amusing cabaret ditty, with a deliberately low key backing, its use of accordion, saxophone and acoustic guitar made the Ants sound like a band of elderly dance hall musicians.

Actually, the worst bands in the world can be heard playing for weddings in top class Parisian hotels, and in comparison, the Ants here sound positively classy.

Adam sang with a dark chuckle in his voice that should have warned critics that there was a strong sense of humour at work and they should not have been so intimidated by the earlier 'Deutchers Girls'. It was the sort of thing one might expect from Ray Davies, or David Bowie in his Decca days and was doubtless intended as a camp joke to be shared among the cognoscenti. It showed that his band were capable of playing in a conventional fashion and were not limited by punk strictures on technical ability. There was a touch of the Loving Spoonfuls about their insouciance.

The B-side – 'Lady' – was an entirely different kettle of suspenders. A fast, powerful performance, it featured some excellent guitar work by Matthew Ashman, winding up an immensely powerful riff over a strong bass line by Andy Warren. The sound of a cane whizzing through the air added an extra dimension to Dave Barbe's stomping, furious drums.

Adam howled, whispered, and hollered his way through a vocal tour de force that expressed an extraordinary number of emotions within the confines of a three minute single. 'Lady' remains one of the great rock statements – brief, pointed and a sharp reminder of the voyeur that resides within us all.

His next single, a year later in 1979 on Do It, was 'Zerox' coupled with 'Whip In My Valise', and once again a vigorous electric guitar motif seemed to announce that Adam was on his way and meant business. He even sang 'Lock up your brain, 'cos I'm here again' as he launched into a menacing opus with violent snare drum explosions piercing a Sex Pistollian melody. In the final bars as the band repeats the final riff there is even a hint of Hawkwind about the swirling and crashing, relieved in the last moments by some harmonics picked from the guitar strings.

Here were the Ants, tougher, more determined, with Adam's lyrics biting deeper, particularly on the head-banging 'Whip In My Valise' in which Mr Ant poses sardonic questions of his lady love, as she joins him in a special 'punishment room'. He announces that he has a stick with lash attached as an implement for punishment concealed in his small portmanteau or kit bag, and before they get down to business he wonders who introduced her to such practices, thinking aloud perhaps that some third party may care to join them and share his or her expertise.

The actual punishment session is represented by the band speeding up the pace, while Dave Barbe's drums grow more heated by the minute.

The grinding guitars and bellowing male chorus show a hint of the Ant music to come in the eighties, but the music of the first phase of Ant creativity was to reach its apogee with the *Dirk Wears White Søx* album released on Do It towards the end of 1979. The line up was once again Dave Barbe (drums), Matthew Ashman (guitars and piano), Andy Warren (bass guitar), and Adam on vocals and some guitars, piano and harmonica. Engineered by Benny King it was recorded at Sound Development in London, and displayed a giant leap forward for Ant music, in terms of lyrics, song structure and recording quality.

The lyrics to the opening cut 'Cartrouble' (Parts 1 & 2)' contained much more narrative and expressed some of the deep seated problems affecting Adam as much as his observation of the ironies of life. It is supposed to be about stripping away the silence surrounding taboo subjects, and one of the examples often cited is his composition 'Catholic Day' about the assassination of President Kennedy in 1963.

Said Adam in an interview: 'To me decadence is getting into drugs, going on stage, completely out of it, surviving on a cult thing and abusing your audience. I find violence decadent. But I've written songs about taboo subjects people interpret as decadent.' He meant sexual deviancy and even the subject of assassinations. It was all a jolly sight more interesting than the rock macho guitar scene that dominated the rock business.

Adam denied that he was trying to be tasteless when he recorded 'Catholic Day' (the second track on side two).

'When he died my mother was in hospital and there were a lot of nuns praying intensely for Kennedy to live. I wanted to write a personal song about his death and what I had felt as a young child. It had been portrayed to me as a romantic death – but it was nothing of the sort. The guy had his brains blown out and I wrote a very brutal song about it. But if you apply a certain degree of lightheartedness to heavy topics then you can take a lot of taboo power out of them. If you can prevent things becoming too serious then there's 'always hope. I think it's a musician's duty to provide some sort of escapism.'

There is neither escapism nor anything

particularly outrageous in the message of *Dirk Wears White Søx*, only a cunning impression of something nagging at the brain, a desire to say something of significance, without actually saying it. Adam sings in anguish and with flaming passion, the band match his contortions, but even on 'Cleopatra', rather than say she was a one for oral sex, Adam tends to say things like 'Cleopatra gave service with a smile'. Rather than breaking down the barriers and bringing filth out into the open for all to see, he seems coy and surreptitious. Indeed through all of Adam's work there is a great absence of discernible filth, smut, blue jokes or foul mouthed muck. His act has always been cleaner than most night club comics, and often a lot funnier.

What *Dirk Wears White Søx* represents is not so much an attack on taboos as simply a band and its leader getting their heads together in a studio and coming up with some exploratory musical performances. It would have been interesting if Adam had recorded this album AFTER *Kings Of The Wild Frontier* for then it would have truly been a bold and dangerous step.

Many feel that 'Cartrouble' is one of the Ants' most interesting creations, opening with a heavy four to the bar beat from Barbe's bass drum, and Ashman's guitar setting a strange brittle mood as Adam sings of awakening in the middle of 'a horrible dream'. The echoing syn drum off-beat gives way to a looser second section as the guitars shift into overdrive, and Adam relaxes his narrative. There is a curious stumble from the drums as the band sets off on its drive around the main theme, and Adam sings in fragments and asides as if he is spending as much time dancing in front of the studio vocal mike as singing.

Matthew's guitar emerges from the left hand speaker of the stereo mix (assuming your speakers are correctly wired) for 'Digital Tenderness' and Adam sustains his declamatory style, incoporating various hiccups and warbles. The exploratory nature of his singing is exemplified by the word chimes he indulges in with the boys in the band, and the song shows off his surprising range and ability to inject meaning into the most unpromising material.

'Nine Plan Failed' is much more interesting than 'Digital Tenderness', however, about the fate of the universal soldier and the stripping of human dignity wrought by war. At least that's my interpretation, open to doubt, question, rebuff and the most heated debate. Adam talks his way through his story with droll choral accompaniment and there is a touch of Bowie about his London boy dénouement.

The 'Day I Met God' *is* outrageous however, and there is a speedy delivery that defies any cries of protest or shock, as Adam mocks the experience of revelation. Malcolm Muggeridge would not be amused. One can only pray that Adam is well insured.

'Table Talk' closes side one and is a slow, atmospheric arrangement with a sophisticated bass line that sings and builds beautifully against some of Barbe's most creative and sensitive drumming on the album. Particularly nice are the neatly placed guitar chords, spreading their tentacles and taking unexpected routes behind the general direction of the theme. Adam's voice spins off into the outer darkness of repeat echo, as he warbles and yodels the spartan but deliciously emotive lyrics, as he catches a frozen moment in time and examines its significance.

What 'Cleopatra' lacks in explicit and graphic description is made up for in other departments, as Adam sings almost like Robert Plant on some of his early Zeppelin albums, with lip curling and subtle arrogance.

'Catholic Day' also recalls an earlier epoch in British rock group history, although it is doubtful if this would be apparent to either Ants or their fans. The merry vocal line, squeaky back up chorus and bitty rhythmic breaks hark back to the late sixties and bands like Skip Bifferty and Glencoe. The use of Kennedy's voice superimposed sounds gimmicky and the hint of smug moralising in the line 'I see the chickens have come home to roost' is unworthy of Adam.

'Never Trust A Man (With Egg On His Face)' is a bizarre fantasy tale, not of perfidy or piddle, but of parricide, and tends to crash about in elephantine fashion. 'Animals And Men' is Adam auctioneering ideas at furious speed with a kind of 'Baggy Trousers' babble of words and voices off stage. Can this be the blueprint for 'Kings Of The Wild Frontier' as he jabbers of the joys of percussion and the voices of mankind?

'Family Of Noise' is a thoroughly enjoyable and extremely witty pastiche of rock group cliches, incorporating riffs and licks from a dozen groups. You can hear a John Bonham style bass drum triplet from Dave Barbe, the tune has overtones of the Beatles' 'Sgt. Pepper', while Adam manages to sound like Steve Marriott, and a whole bunch of Cockney soul singers. The final throwaway line 'In Croydon' which is where rock salvation is supposed to take place, is wonderful.

This album, packed with subtleties and made all the more effective by its occasional rough edges, and raw studio sound, is in many ways an album for life, which alone should have established Adam's place in the higher echelons as a songwriter and performer of immense relevance and importance.

'The Idea' which concludes this palette of dark and mysterious colours, is a final splash of artistic expression as the guitar and bass lines work against each other in apparently conflicting roles but swiftly lock into swirling torrents of sound flecked by bell chimes tolling behind Adam's dissertation on a theme about a disco communion.

After this triumph another single version of 'Cartrouble' was released in March 1980 together with 'Kick' recorded by the new Ants and released on Do It.

But the great leap forward (or backwards, depending on your critical stance) came with 'Kings Of The Wild Frontier' their first CBS single, coupled with 'Press Darlings' and released in July 1980. The immediate impact of the new Ants sound was astounding. The engineering and mixing did not detract from or diminish Adam's vocal status, but the rhythm section, from being a personal dialogue between Andy Warren and Dave Barbe with much room for improvisation, had turned into a thunderous juggernaut, an orchestra of tympani and jungle drums.

There was much tongue in cheek humour as Adam and his new cohorts whooped, danced and screamed around a camp fire burning the relics of the past. They sounded like they had never sounded before - as if they were having enormous fun and a right royal good time.

For this was Ant music with the new ingredient - Marco power. His guitar clanked and howled, picking on harmless notes with the tenderness and care of King Kong prodding Fay Wray.

This indeed was the Ant manifesto, proclaiming the slogans that were to assail the ears of journalists, disc jockeys, and all keen collectors of pop discs. 'Ant people are the warriors!' he yelled, and for good measure added 'Ant music is the banner!' There was no arguing with facts like these. The hordes flocked to his banner, rushing over the brow of the hill to surprise Adam and his little group of followers where they had until now been quietly turning water into wine and performing minor miracles of communication. Now the masses diverted off the motorways of mediocrity and headed towards this strangely clad prophet, until now parked in the lay-bys of rhythm.

The redskins may have suffered from centuries of taming, but Adam had suffered from a couple of years of bad reviews and now he could not resist getting his own back. The B-side of the single was dedicated to a good humoured but nevertheless biting get back at his critics, taking the unprecedented step of naming such rock writers as Nick Kent and Gary Bushell. 'And what's more, they tell fibs,' Adam added, to show how silly it all was and that he hoped bygones would be dumped and hands shaken all round. Whatever else the track proved, it showed the new Ants could rock as well as beat the jungle path to their new SOUND.

'Dog Eat Dog' was the next single in the procession of hits that Adam launched upon us all, and when ever 1980 is discussed this will be one of the tracks used to identify the times and people. The rumbling introduction and lightly pounding beat reminded me of Cannibal and the Headhunters and 'Land Of A Thousand Dances' but the spirit was all Adam, and the slamming accents breaking up the chants of the warriors was very daring, as were the vocal lines spoiling over into the next chorus and making the most unexpected entrances and departures. The whole effect was to break the stranglehold of pop and rock music production, tradition and convention. It was a wonderful burst of enterprise that worked first time.

Links with the past were maintained on the B-side however, with a new version of a song that had been a mainstay of the Ant stage act, and was one of Adam's own favourites, the grinding, bumping and menacing 'Physical (You're So)' which showed that in order to break with tradition you need to understand it very well. This was sixties college gig rock drenched in sweat, bodies, beer, students, bouncers, jobsworths, roadies, soundchecks, overflowing loos and broken windows.

As Adam explained he performed his strip tease on this number simply because he was hot. Well, why not? If you were playing in some filthy cellar for £5 a night, you might be tempted to divest yourself of your garments and utter a cry of despair. The screaming feedback can best be interpreted as a plea for love and attention – or at least another pint of lager.

'Antmusic' which followed was the most

ethnic of Adam's ventures into the music of African tribesmen, the most obviously influenced by the clashing of Zulu spears on shields and the beating of stout cudgels on the heads of their adversaries. One could imagine something similar being played during the battle of Rorke's Drift.

It was heartening that pop ears accustomed to the bland bump of disco should be able to accept the sophisticated contrapuntal polyrhythms incorporated from the offset as Terry Lee Miall and Merrick clicked their sticks in authentic fashion in the opening bars – normally regarded as the make or break moment in pop single making. The symphonic nature of Marco's guitar and Kevin Mooney's bass backcloth helped create a wide screen image, a sort of cinematic exploration of the kingdom of the Ants as they sang of the creatures' remarkable ability to survive even the most careless form of surgery.

'Fall In' had Adam, rock singer, in full flight, with loads of echo, and all the teen appeal of a bobbysoxer calling the shots at a village hop. Gone by now was the menace and introspection of *Dirk* – this was the King letting his curls down and doing the bop in front of the trestle table loaded with orange juice.

If Ant fans had complained of a paucity of material in the past, now there was a flood with the release of his second album, *Kings Of The Wild Frontier*, in the autumn.

Here were all the singles but some more material that was to provide the basis for the extensive touring the band undertook in the wake of their success; pieces like 'Feed Me To The Lions' and the Shadows-styled 'Los Rancheros' which paid homage to Clint Eastwood, Charles Bronson and all the cowboys of movie mythology. Here was Marco at his most magnificent, with vibrato slung low, and Adam whooping and hollering his way through the tumble weed, in a cloud of dust and bullets.

By now Col. Tom would have had Adam signed up for his first Western, as the tin star sheriff with a team of cowpokes to hustle out of town. British rock stars do not good actors make-up until now.

'Ants Invasion' is a strange and powerful story of fear and loathing, as the young Ant trembles on the brink of making a decision that will affect his whole life. Marco's guitar squeaks like a thousand ants rubbing their antennae together and one imagines Adam on the doorstep of the Great Manager in the sky wondering whether to go in and sign away his inheritance for a mess of potage.

'Killer In The Home' has equally doomy overtones with an open guitar chordal backing that recalls some of Pete Townshend's work on 'Tommy'. Adam is haunted by the spectre of the warrior he must face and fight and by the subtle word play one can detect the inner Stuart Goddard calling desperately for help from inside his carefully constructed vision of Adam. The ultimate battle between the two personalities holds a fatal fascination.

Some have brutally called many of the less obviously popular items on *Kings Of The Wild Frontier* rubbish. But this is patently unfair and inaccurate. 'The Magnificent Five' may not be his most outstanding work, but 'Don't Be Square (Be There)' is rich in direct rock appeal and amusing asides. The riff is the closest to R&B and the Yardbirds that the Ants have yet reached, with a thoroughly groovy ascending guitar riff, and some surreal interpolation from Adam as he suddenly harkens back to the recent past with an out of context yell of 'Dirk Wears White Søx'. The effect is of two juke boxes battling it out at opposite ends of the bar.

The hijinks and Gang Show exuberance of 'Jolly Roger' may well offend the seeker of gloom and significance, but it reflected another phase of Adam's interest in the heroic figures of history. He compared the pirates to the red indians, as youthful figures filled with pride. One wonders if he is aware that buccaneers had their origins in sailors who took to curing pork meat, then switched to piracy when the bottom fell out of the pig market. But then butchery and piracy have always been closely linked.

Adam concluded his overview of civilisation with 'Making History' and 'The Human Beings'. Not great songs, but delivered with the same passion and sincerity that has marked all of Adam's work since the beginning of Ants.

Kings Of The Wild Frontier was in many ways a strange, bold album of concentrated will power and combined expertise, that richly deserved its nine-month (plus) stay in the charts and its huge sales. It could be said it sold on the strength of Adam's teen appeal, his looks, and all the paraphernalia of make-up, mystique and deliberate sloganeering. But without the music, and without the Ants, and their backup team of engineers, there could have been no Adam, and no phenomenon.

It was the music that made the breakthrough, and the dedication to a new sound that would cut away the encrusted grime of ages past.

In 1981 Adam proved that he could sustain his output with 'Stand And Deliver' written by Marco and Adam and released in May as a single that would confound the critics who warned he could not keep up the pace. It went straight to number one - of course. With a posthorn gallop and a merry eighteenth-century cry from dandy Adam, it was an unashamed showbiz production, on which Adam sounded like he had shed ten years and was a cheeky young brat straight from school entertaining for the mums and dads and kids at the holiday camp concert, his voice breaking, and desperate to win the box of chocolates.

It was a stunningly exuberant whirligig of whistles, whoops, neighing horses, and the sound of highwaymen beating on the carriage doors to the high pitched screams of the coach passengers. 'It'll be a sad day when showbiz is a dirty word,' said Adam cheerfully to the *Melody Maker* in April that year. It was difficult not to smile at Adam's cry of 'Stand and delivah!' which was of course not necessarily about highway robbery but about youth and its mad pursuit of stale, scruffy fashion, when they could be joining the 'insect nation', and dressing flash. He backed up this profound statement with the expressive postscript 'A diddly qua qua' of deep significance to us all.

Just in case there were still Ant fans from the old days standing somewhat disconsolate in their attics with dusty whips and cobwebbed copies of 'Lady', the B-side was 'Beat My Guest', a super fast piece of Flagellism 'n' Yodels. The band steams with unrestrained fervour, Marco's guitar work complete with wolf whistle effects, and jams safe in the knowledge that this is a B-side and the critics and the fans' parents won't be listening too hard.

How hard will they listen in the future? Whatever the Red Indian, the Punk, the Pirate, the Highwayman, the Prince Charming springs on us next, we dare not fail to take heed. Ant music undoubtedly has the power and, one is tempted to say, is the banner.

Chapter Nine

THE ANT MUST GO ON

Early on during the Ants' rise to public acclaim they ran into the sharp end of rock when they were involved in a punch up at BBC TV's *Top Of The Pops* during a recording of the show. It happened when Jimmy Lydon, of the 4Be2s and brother of John Lydon, clashed with the band outside the studios. A report in the London *News Standard* told how members of the Ants and the 4Be2s fought after a girl had been pushed down a flight of stairs. Police were called and no arrests were made. Adam would not comment after the incident, and a spokesman said he wouldn't want to give the other band any more publicity.

The incident served to underline Adam's dislike of the growing violence that was affecting the rock scene and his desire to counteract its influence.

Much of the point of the Ant campaign was to supply a healthy alternative for kids to the 'Oi' music movement, and to counteract the decadence of violence. He found it as depressing as the drug culture of traditional rock.

Said Adam: 'Bands were getting into drug life styles, producing esoteric albums where the audience didn't know whether they were coming or going. The bands wore dull, grey clothes because they were existentialist and deep and were being dropped left, right and centre by record companies. You can only fool so many of the people so much of the time. Audiences want to see some action.'

Adam insists that audiences should be taken out of grim reality and given not only value for money but an event they will never forget. He regards this as a challenge and crusade. 'A lot of artists tend to think they are gracing their audiences just by being in town. The majority of young people I think are above violence and degradation. All I fight for is my music. I abhor violence in all its forms.' He knew that some fans were actually scared to attend Ant performances because of their fears of being beaten up.

Adam is against what he astutely calls 'dole queue martyrdom' and he knows by experience, from his illness, from mental crack ups, from being criticised, ignored and dumped, that ultimately, only the inner self can fight for self respect, a sense of purpose and achievement and a form of happiness if not pure contentment.

It is unlikely that Adam Ant will ever be wholly content. He is far too intelligent to allow himself that luxury. He will change his mind about his future direction and completely astonish everybody surrounding him. This much one can predict simply by observing his track record.

'People don't know what's coming next. I don't know what's coming next.'

In March 1981 Gary Tibbs, who had been a member of Roxy Music, took over from Kevin Mooney on bass, just in time to rehearse for the group's Stand And Deliver Tour which was hailed as a 'thank you' to all the fans and new sex people who had made the success story possible. At the same time *Kings Of The Wild Frontier* went back to number one in the album charts for the second time.

After the British tour the band went to America, where a flurry of transatlantic interviews helped pave their way. The album was not a huge chart hit there, but the reaction to their live performances was immensely encouraging. They played at the Roxy in Los Angeles and a whole host of fellow Britons went to cheer Adam on to new success. Both Elton John and Rod Stewart were in the audience at the famous club and Britt Eckland was there to check out Adam's sex appeal.

In New York the town went Ant crazy and once again fellow countrymen turned up to lend moral support. One of the surprise visitors was Pete Townshend of the Who, actually seen dancing to a wild version of 'Dog Eat Dog', when the band played at the Ritz. Later the Ants were booked into the Palladium, a dusty old theatre full of faded glories in Manhattan. It used to be an opera house and was relaunched as a rock venue by the Rolling Stones when they played there a couple of years earlier, and the dirt was wiped from the long neglected chandeliers.

This time the fans were older than they were in England and there were none of the hysterical mobbing scenes Adam had begun to enjoy back home. They listened calmly enough, but liked what they heard. For by now, after hard touring, the 'new' band was well and truly broken in. It had become a tight professional act, with excellent sound and lights, to match the very best American rock audiences demand in presentation.

Said US rock critic Aaron B. Zeigfield: 'No way was this the kind of ragged UK punk rock we had come to expect. This reminded me of Canned Heat or Steppenwolf.' American rock critics can be somewhat old fashioned in their outlook.

Audiences demanded encores however and even let fly with the occasional cry of 'right on' and 'really neat'. Said Adam, tired but happy, with the greasepaint trickling over his brow: 'This was a very encouraging start, but we're not getting too cocky yet. The audiences really enjoyed themselves.'

The Americans were most impressed by pictures of Adam that had been taken with Princess Margaret when he signed his autograph for her at the London Palladium. If the Ants were good enough for royalty, they were good enough for New York.

They returned to Britain on April 27, 1981 and were plunged next day into playing a special charity concert at London's Venue, in aid of the Multiple Sclerosis appeal, sharing the bill with Dexy's Midnight Runners, long favourites with Adam, and Lene Lovich. At the same time Marco Pirroni celebrated his twenty-second birthday, as well as a year of contributing to Adam's enormous musical triumph.

In July the band began work on the next LP after completing and showing the video for 'Stand And Deliver'. 'Prince Charming' was then scheduled as the follow up.

In twelve months the Ants had transformed the face of British pop and given it new hope and a sense of direction. The invasion was over and the occupation had begun.

Release Date	Title	Label	Cat. no.
March 10 1978	*Jubilee - Outrageous Film Soundtrack* album (two tracks - Plastic Surgery/Deutscher Girls)	E.G./Polydor	Polydor Deluxe 2302079
October 1978	Young Parisians/Lady single	Decca	Decca F13803
July 6 1979	Zerox/Whip In My Valise single	Do It	DO IT DUN 8
November 30 1979	*Dirk Wears White Søx* album	Do It	DO IT RIDE 3
March 3 1980	Cartrouble/Kick single	Do It	DO IT DUN 10
July 1980	Kings Of The Wild Frontier/Press Darlings single	CBS	CBS 8877
October 3 1980	Dog Eat Dog/Physical (You're So) single	CBS	CBS 9039
November 1980	*Kings Of The Wild Frontier* album	CBS	CBS 84549
November 1980	Antmusic/Fall In single	CBS	CBS 9352
May 1 1981	Stand And Deliver/Beat My Guest	CBS	CBS A 1065

Jubilee - Outrageous Films Soundtrack album
E.G./Polydor   Polydor Deluxe 2302079

Recorded: between July 1977 and September 1977

Released: March 10 1978

Just two tracks: 1. Plastic Surgery
2. Deutscher Girls

Adam & The Ants Personnel featured on:

1. *Plastic Surgery*

Words/Music	Adam Ant
Jordan	vocals
Andy Warren	bass/vocals
Adam Ant	vocals/guitar
Dave Barbe	drums
Johnny Bivouac	guitar/vocals
Produced by	Danny Beckerman and Will Malone
Engineered by	Will Malone at Chappells Studios

2. *Deutscher Girls*

Words/Music	Adam Ant
Johnny Bivouac	guitar/vocals
Andy Warren	bass/vocals
Adam Ant	vocals/guitar
Dave Barbe	drums
Jordan	vocals
Produced by	Guy Ford and Adam & The Ants and Don Hawkins at Air Studios

Young Parisians/Lady single   Decca   Decca F 13803

Recorded: August 1978 at Basing St. Studios, London

Released: October 1978

Adam & The Ants Personnel:

Words/Music	Adam Ant
Andy Warren	bass
Adam Ant	vocals/guitar
Dave Barbe	drums
Matthew Ashman	guitar/piano
Jo Julian	piano
Greg Mason	saxophone
Produced by	Joseph Julian and Adam Ant
Engineered by	Joseph Julian

Highest Position in chart: 7

First entered chart: January 1981

Cartrouble/Kick single   Do It   DO IT DUN 10

Recorded: February 18/19 1980 at Rockfield Studios, Monmouth

Released: March 3 1980

Adam & The Ants Personnel:

Words/Music	Adam Ant
Adam Ant	vocals/guitar
Terry Lee Miall	drums
Marco Pirroni	guitar/vocals
Produced by	Hugh Jones

Highest position in chart: 38

Kings Of The Wild Frontier/Press Darlings single
CBS   CBS 8877

Recorded: April 1980 at Matrix Studios, London

Released: July 1980

Number sold: over 500,000 (gold)

Adam & The Ants Personnel:

Words/Music	Ant/Marco (Press Darlings by Adam Ant)

Adam Ant	vocals/guitar
Terry Lee Miall	drums
Marco Pirroni	guitar/vocals
Merrick	drums
Kevin Mooney	bass/vocals

Produced by	Chris Hughes
Engineered by	Simon Heyworth

Highest position in chart: 1

When first released in July 1980 it charted at no. 48 after one week and then dropped out. As the single was not deleted, it later entered the chart on February 19 1981 and rose to the top.

Dog Eat Dog/Physical (You're So) single

CBS   CBS 9039

Recorded: August 1980 at Rockfield Studios, Monmouth

Released: October 3 1980

Number sold: 100,000+ (gold)

Adam & The Ants Personnel:

Dog Eat Dog
   written by   Adam Ant/Marco Pirroni
Physical written by   Adam Ant

Adam Ant   vocals/guitar
Terry Lee Miall   drums
Marco Pirroni   guitar/vocals
Merrick   drums
Kevin Mooney   bass/vocals

Produced by   Chris Hughes
Engineered by   Hugh Jones

Highest position in chart: 3

First entered chart: October 7 1980

'Physical' was originally recorded by the old band in
August 1979 at the same time as the *Dirk Wears White
Søx* album, but was not used until Chris Hughes
remixed it for Do It Records and they secretly released
it as the B-side to the first 3,000 copies of the 'Zerox'
single in July 1979.

Kings Of The Wild Frontier album   CBS   CBS 84549

Recorded: August 1980 at Rockfield Studios, Monmouth

Released: November 1980

Number sold: 750,000 (double platinum)

Number of weeks in chart: 36 weeks (still in top 10 in July 1981)

Track Listing:

Side One: Dog Eat Dog
'Antmusic'
Feed Me To The Lions
Los Rancheros
Ants Invasion
Killer In The Home

Side Two: Kings Of The Wild Frontier
The Magnificent Five
Don't Be Square (Be There)
Jolly Roger
Making History
The Human Beings

Adam & The Ants Personnel:

Songs written by	Adam Ant/Marco Pirroni
Marco Pirroni	guitar/vocals
Adam Ant	vocals/guitar
Kevin Mooney	bass/vocals
Terry Lee Miall	drums
Merrick	drums
Produced by	Chris Hughes
Engineered by	Hugh Jones

Highest position in chart: 1

First entered chart: November 11 1980

Antmusic/Fall In single   CBS   CBS 9352

Recorded: August and October 1980

Released: November 1980

Number sold: 100,000+ (gold)

Adam & The Ants Personnel:

    'Antmusic'
      Words/Music   Adam Ant/Marco Pirroni
    'Fall In'
      Words/Music   Adam Ant/Lester Square

Adam Ant	vocals/guitar
Terry Lee Miall	drums
Marco Pirroni	guitar/vocals
Merrick	drums
Kevin Mooney	bass/vocals
Produced by	Chris Hughes and remixed at Matrix Studios

Highest position in chart: 2

First entered chart: December 2 1980

This single was only kept from the no. 1 spot by John Lennon's 'Imagine'.

Stand And Deliver/Beat My Guest single

CBS   CBS A1065

Recorded: February 9 1981 at Townhouse Studios

Released: May 1 1981

Number sold: 500,000+ (gold)

Adam & The Ants Personnel:

Stand And Deliver
   Words/Music   Ant/Pirroni
Beat My Guest
   Words/Music   Adam Ant

Adam Ant   vocals/guitar
Gary Tibbs   bass
Merrick   drums
Terry Lee Miall   drums
Marco Pirroni   guitar/vocals

Produced by   Chris Hughes
Engineered by   Alan Douglas

Highest position in chart: 1

First entered chart: May 1981

STOP PRESS:

Prince Charming single   CBS Records